Father Candido Amantini

Father Candido Amantini

The Wisdom and Faith of the Exorcist
and Servant of God

by
Andrea Maniglia

Foreword by Fr. Cliff Ermatinger

2025
Slaying Dragons Press

"Father Candido's blessing":

> May the Lord Jesus be with you always.
> May He walk before you to guide you,
> May He be behind you to protect you,
> May He dwell within you to guard you,
> May He be above you to enlighten you.
> Amen.

Which Father Amorth preferred to say in Latin:

> *Dominus noster Jesus Christus, apud nos sit ut nos defendat,*
> *intra nos sit ut nos conservet, ante nos sit ut nos ducat,*
> *post nos sit ut nos custodiat,*
> *super nos sit ut nos benedicat, liberet et sanctificet:*
> *Qui cum Patre et Spiritu Sancto vivit et regnat in saecula saeculorum.*
> *Amen.*

In deference to the constitutions of Pope Urban VIII, the facts recounted in this volume are to be given only the intended faith from the testimony adduced, and it is not intended to preempt, in any way, the judgment that Holy Mother Church will give on the main character of this book and the facts concerning him.

TABLE OF CONTENTS

ACKNOWLEDGEMENTS

Before delving into these reflections of ours, let me again express my sincere thanks to the Postulator of the Cause for the beatification and canonization of the Servant of God, Dr. Paolo Vilotta, to the *Father Candido Amantini* Prayer Group and, in particular, to Professor Mother Annamaria Valli, O.S.B. a.p., for accepting the invitation to curate the preface to the Italian edition of this volume.

These pages have not been conceived as a true biography; instead, they are created to offer readers and devotees of the Servant of God elements interspersed between historical and biographical ones and some theological and spiritual ones. These have been stitched together; indeed, it is better to specify that they have been juxtaposed. These pages do not, therefore, constitute a study of the figure of the Servant of God, but are meant to offer a little essay regarding the life of the exorcist of the Holy Stairs, on the occasion of the XXV anniversary of his death, celebrated in September 2017.

These pages, it should be pointed out, do not exhaust the knowledge of a singular, complex, and in many ways, interesting and *exciting* story.

Writing and delving into this story has been both delightful and comforting to me because his holy life embodies ideas and patterns that amount to a program of highest asceticism.

I have been writing about Amantini for years, probably also reiterating the usual concepts. But I write, however, in the awareness and with the desire to remain — to use an image — in the shadow line of a door that remains open but which can never be fully crossed.

This man's life remains a mystery — a mystery of charity!

Andrea Maniglia

AUTHOR'S NOTE

THIS BOOK, after updates and supplements, has drawn from various articles and considerations published a few years ago on the Facebook page and website of the National Papaboys Association (Associazione Nazionale Papaboys).[1] I was asked, subsequently, to carry out this work on our Servant of God and to explore his personage even more, which I gladly accomplished despite the many limitations.

Thanks to Edizioni San Paolo,[2] this book is now being resubmitted, which I hope will help the reader to deepen his knowledge of this amazing and extraordinary figure of a man and religious who was "a priest after God's own heart." It is the continuation — certainly still incomplete — of the previous popular biographies I have written on the exorcist

---

[1] The Associazione Nazionale Papaboys is an Italian youth association founded in 2004 at the request of Pope John Paul II. Its goal is to bring the youth closer to the heart of the Church through participation in various events which are centered in prayer, community, and engagement with ecclesial events. It emerged from the enthusiasm that followed the World Youth Day events. The mission of the Papaboys is to evangelize and to bring the message of Jesus Christ to the youth, especially to those who are away from the Church. It has spread from Italy to many other countries. -Ed.

[2] The publisher of the original Italian edition. -Ed.

of Rome. The first, *Alla Scala Santa avete un santo! Andate da lui!* (At the Holy Stairs you have a saint! Go to him!) published in 2012, in Italian, by Velar (Blue series, Messaggeri d'amore). The second, *Sull'uscio di casa* (On the Doorstep) published in 2015, in Italian, by Tau in the *I capolavori* series. The third, *Come melograno fiorito,* (As a Flowering Pomegranate), published in 2017 by Edizioni Segno.

This book does not pretend to be exhaustive or to give definitive answers to certain questions about the figure of our Servant of God. The purpose is to provide some indications in this regard. We might say that this book is not a *book*, but a *call,* an encounter with Someone through someone. Without going into a properly critical and analytical historiographical analysis, not least because one has to wait, for this, for the release of the *Positio super virtutibus,*[3] I wanted to indicate ways for further study and above all to arouse the desire for greater knowledge.

Before the figure of the saints, after all, the desire for knowledge becomes a desire to imitate.

The simple, humble, and joyful holiness of Amantini proposes, in this world of ours, with particular effectiveness, the spirit of the Gospel, which only the little ones, the disciples of the Kingdom, can embody. The Church's recognition of his holiness will certainly, even now, be an impetus, particularly for the consecrated, to return to that demanding simplicity of the Gospel, as Pope Francis has reminded us, and to make a sacrifice of one's life, in humility and gladness, for the glory of the Lord and the service of one's neighbor. It must be reiterated again that his human and supernatural personality and work are still far from being adequately studied. Many agree that, unfortunately,

> important personalities in the history of the Passionist Congregation, [...] are not studied

---

[3] The key document which summarizes the virtues, holiness, and miracles of one potentially to be declared a "blessed" or "saint." -Ed.

in depth by young Passionist religious or those who are part of the Passionist Family. [Instead, it is important] to revisit the person and life of the people God has raised up in the history of the Church, to realize, thus, a kind of dialogue between the past and the present that always reveals new aspects of the wonderful work done by God in his saints. (Father Adolfo Lippi c.p.)

I would like to point out, moreover, that these various publications concerning the figure of the exorcist of Rome, expanded and enriched one after the other, as I have been rightly reproached, should have come out a long time ago, but it was not possible for me to do for various reasons. Unfortunately, this delay allowed someone to print "pirated" editions, which did not help to present a fair figure of Amantini.

The information contained in my work then, appropriately supplemented with other documents, have been elaborated to put the reader in a position to be able to follow the story of our Servant of God and to be able to understand a little more of his personality that touches, without a shadow of a doubt, the highest peaks of mysticism. His is the experience of a profoundly human man; a true experience, rooted in the encounter with God, capable of touching with strength and hope those who suffer, even in the most serious (and desperate) situations of pain.

It is people like these, after all, who make holiness something concretely great. It is people like these that stir the innocent desire to return to the Gospel.

It is people such as these — people whose serene voice we cherish in our memory, united to that courage that has overcome death — that forbid us to let the mystery of Christ fall like a meteorite before us without provoking anything in our hearts, or without it provoking questions in our minds.

I sincerely hope to help the reader truly grasp Amantini's message; to understand, moreover, that Candido Amantini was truly and fully a man; not a semblance of a man or a man *in parenthesis*. Rather, he was a creature whose humanity is truly exalted.

I sincerely hope to help the reader also grasp the deepest yearning of the exorcist of Rome — that of knowing that he was intimately, profoundly, totally, body and soul, associated with the Divine Will, on the way towards that goal, of which he already had a foretaste in life, ardently desiring.

FOREWORD

THE TAXI DRIVER pulled up to the majestic doors of St. John Lateran on a hot July 13th in 2012. He deposited me and my luggage there an hour or two after my plane landed in Rome. My mind was foggy and still adjusting but I had arrived in time for the official opening of the beatification process of the Servant of God, Candido Amantini. Present were some old friends and comrades in spiritual arms, Father Gabriele Amorth, Father Francesco Bamonte, their respective team members, and a modest menagerie of other exorcists, clergy, Passionist Fathers, and journalists.

Before us sat a panel of theological experts, the postulator for the cause and, of course, the devil's advocate who worked to ensure that the process would be objective and include any discoverable and relevant negative information for a more complete picture of the candidate for beatification. Informal and lighthearted mention was made of the curious role of a *devil's* advocate in the beatification process of an *exorcist.*

At a time when many often look to exorcists as a form of oracle, such a phenomenon reveals a certain tenuous grasp of those sources that Christ has given us to reveal everything we need to know for what really matters: namely, Sacred Scripture, Tradition, and the perennial liturgy which has been handed down to us from the Apostles. People who read books by and about exorcists are often attracted to the extraordinary abilities that demons seem to exhibit. Yet there is nothing extraordinary about angels[1] working within the limits of their own nature. For us it may seem extraordinary and otherworldly, and it certainly is, but addicts of such sensationalism and those afflicted with such morbid curiosity would have come away from the official opening of the beatification process with a degree of disappointment. There was no mention of those anecdotes, just the facts of the life of the Servant of God and the shape the thorough and objective process would take, which was no different than any other candidate's process.

A reader of this book whose penchant tends towards sensationalism may be equally disappointed. It is easy to blame Hollywood for engendering this unhealthy fascination, but such human weakness predates modern means of mass communication. In the Gospel of Luke 4:41, in which Christ exorcises a possessed man, the demon reveals His identity, yet Christ rebukes him and refuses to let him speak further; not because what he said was untrue, but rather owing to our Lord's concern for us and those immediate witnesses of the event. He would rather we *not* get information - not even *true* information - from demons, but instead that we look to the authentic means of revelation and its arbiter, the Holy Church, for what we need to know with regard to doctrine.

Another result of our fallenness is the human tendency to look to somebody in a worse situation to justify one's own dilapidated spiritual life. Many who, out of morbid curiosity, are attracted to anecdotal evidence of demonic activity recounted by exorcists on YouTube, often fail to recognize the demonic that is front and center in their own lives. Infernal circus sideshows can easily distract us from our own attachments to sin. On the other hand, some people fear the

---

[1] Demons are *fallen* angels, retaining their angelic nature, though lacking grace.

devil more than they fear God. A young man once told me that the thing he feared most in life was demonic possession. I told him he was crazy, of course. In terms of worst-case scenarios, that's nowhere near the top of that infelicitous heap. An infinitely worse scenario is that in which God is offended, namely through sin. The loss of the life of grace constitutes an existential disaster for the soul, a triumph for the devil, and, worst of all, an offence against the Almighty who is unbounded Goodness itself. This last aspect is the worst part of sin, for it is an assault on God's extrinsic glory and brings Him sorrow. If people took this to heart, there would be less need for the extraordinary means that the Church provides through exorcism.

Perhaps it is the ugliness of possession and the hideous things demons foist upon the bodies of the afflicted that distract people from working on their own souls and giving God glory with their words, thoughts, and actions. The way out of this disorder is to immerse oneself, as this Servant of God did, in the Passion of Christ, allowing one's heart and mind to be configured to that of Christ. The Passion of Christ then, with all the trials and grief and sorrow that it brings, is the only path to happiness ... and Fr. Candido Amantini lived those truths in his own flesh and soul.

What we see in this book are a series of theological statements to begin each chapter and then an explanation of how Candido Amantini exemplified that theological statement with his heroically virtuous life. None of what is contained in those statements ought to be foreign to the faithful follower of Christ, rather they should make up our life: centered on the Eucharist, true devotion to Mary, love of silence and prayer, and exercise of spiritual combat, *for our struggle is not against flesh and blood,...but against the spiritual forces of evil in the heavenly realms* (Eph. 6:12).

Although there is some mention in these pages of extraordinary phenomena, divine and demonic, what is truly extraordinary is the degree with which Fr. Candido Amantini lived virtue: namely, his love for Christ, his configuration with Christ Crucified, and his love for souls. That's what separates the saint from the mediocre soul, radical following of Christ without compromises or calculations. That's part of the role of any of the beatified and canonized: they not only reveal to us that holiness is possible, but they also show us how to attain it. Candido died with a Rosary in his hands, not as a mere exterior devotion, but with the entirety of the Gospel that it contains — in his hands, mind, and heart — for it had formed him to be the man of God that he was and remains in everlasting life.

Fr. Cliff Ermatinger

INTRODUCTION

HOLINESS IS CLOSE to us; it is the attire of the ordinary and is within our reach. It makes no sense for a Christian to say, "This is not the right stuff for me!" On the contrary, it is the right stuff for all of us!

The charm of holiness is enchantment, which is why there is nothing more beautiful in the world than the face and smile of a *saint*. We, who often live out the faith in a primarily rational manner, should allow ourselves to be challenged by the charm of holiness.

Many witnesses, also because of this, when speaking of the Servant of God Candido Amantini, recall how his distinguishing trait was his smile. He was always serene — a model of tranquility. The challenges, sufferings, and frequent mortifications did not darken the light of hope that shone from his smile.

Father Candido was a *free* person because he lived in full communion with the Lord; that is why he did not let himself be oppressed by anguish, but lived in that exquisitely evangelical joy, which, as Benedict XVI stated, is a sign of grace. One who is serene from the bottom of his heart, one who has suffered without losing joy, is not far from the God of the Gospel, from the Spirit of God, who is the Spirit of eternal joy.[1]

The Church, unfortunately, even today allows itself to fall into crises and stagnation when joy dies on the faces of her children. Each of us is always called to show this joy, a joy that is firmly rooted in the *Jesus event.* Looking at the holiness and joy with which Father Candido lived his life and his specific baptismal vocation, we, too, cannot help but be wonderfully attracted to it and consequently facilitated to respond to the *universal call to holiness.* He could be compared to those daring people who, with tenacity and courage, go against the current of this world, committed to great ideals, for an equally great love that never wanes, without worrying about worldly trends.

Today more than ever I am deeply convinced that Father Candido Amantini, the exorcist of Rome, has never crossed the threshold of the Pontifical Sanctuary of the Holy Stairs in Rome; that is, he has never left it. Even after his death, he is always there, between the sacristy and the St. Sylvester altar, among his cell and the corridors of the convent. His presence is alive. It can be felt. Stopping near the altar rail where he used to celebrate Mass, one can close his eyes and see him again as he raises the Sacred Host, or as he traces, almost as a smile, a broad cross over the world and over each of us.

I met Father Candido Amantini while going about my way, by chance, almost providentially, one ordinary day in 2012. He told me about a God who cannot be studied in books, but who is encountered in life and who is loved in life. A God who is crazy with love: a love that is completely free, of extreme giving as true love. God's love is *God-sized*

---

[1] Ratzinger, J. (2008). The God of Jesus Christ: Meditations on the Triune God (Brian McNeil, Trans.; pp. 111–113). Ignatius Press.

precisely because His is a love without measure. For true love begins where nothing more is asked in return, and its culmination and apex consist in suffering and dying for the other. Father Candido

> has guided us in the arena of history, revealing to us the speed of the Gospel and the passion of the Church that travels the streets of the world with the Cross of the dead and risen Christ. (Monsignor Cosmo F. Ruppi)

The life of our Servant of God has presented, by unveiling them, two aspects: humility and simplicity. These were two fundamental notes of Amantini's entire human and spiritual experience, which revealed his true face and constituted the atmosphere in which all other virtues subsequently developed. They highlighted his being and way of acting in everyday life and made him lovable and easily approachable at all times. There was nothing sensational, just an extraordinary life in the ordinariness of history. The virtue of obedience also shines in Father Candido: one could speak of "obedience of faith" in the Pauline sense, since obedience and faith are intrinsically connected and practically identified with one another. The entire life of the Servant of God was an act of faith — one translated into a concrete and active obedience to the will of God.

Father Candido was a man of silence. Pope Benedict XVI, in his message for the Day of Communications, spoke on this theme, stating:

> Silence, then, gives rise to even more active communication, requiring sensitivity and a capacity to listen that often makes manifest the

true measure and nature of the relationships involved.[2]

Father Candido, before being an exorcist, had chosen to immerse himself in the silence of Passionist spirituality, but God was thinking otherwise for him by putting him in the forefront of the fight against the powers of evil.

He looked at every man with eyes of compassion and love, with that same intensity with which Jesus himself loved the crowds who approached him. He did not shut himself up in his cell, but sought immortal souls, freeing them from the chains of sin. That is why the figure of Christ, the Redeemer of man, who never tires of teaching the ways of spiritual and human rebirth, is at the root of Amantini's spirituality.

Holiness, as we will never tire of repeating, is apparently ordinary, but supported by sound virtues. The saint, after all, is never a museum piece. He is a living man who adheres to God and, in this way, adheres to that vocation on which and for which his heart is built.

The world still needs, especially today, the "spectacle of holiness," as Gustave Bardy refers to it when speaking of the early centuries of Christianity. That is, a fully human holiness, as fully human saints did not need to forget or deny any of their humanity. Adrienne von Speyr wrote that

> the saints are a demonstration of the possibility of Christianity; thus, they can be guides on a road to God's charity that seems otherwise impossible.

For this reason, holiness is not an exceptional fact in the Church. It plays a particular role and becomes almost like a pedagogical paradigm: in each saint, the Christian glimpses

---

[2] Message Of His Holiness Pope Benedict XVI for the 46th World Communications Day – *Silence and Word: Path of Evangelization*, Sunday, 20 May 2012. Vatican.va

the structure of his own figure; he glimpses what he is called to be. That is why in the early days of Christianity it was recommended to "seek the faces of the saints every day and draw comfort from their sermons."[3]

In studying the figure of our Servant of God, I have come to understand that the real problem of Christian holiness is not the choice of a particular attitude to have in the world, but knowing how to recognize, in the toil of each day, that *unique event*, that truly special Something that happened and that was freely given to us. Therein lies the key: leaning on and adhering to that Someone who appeared in the flesh and saved me. For this reason, holiness is living within history: holiness is not an escape from the world, from life, or from reality! This is why Georges Bernanos wrote in 1937 that

> the saints are those who maintain that interior
> life without which humanity will destroy itself
> to the point of dying.

We are made for great things, for profound joys that are born from prophetic viewpoints, high ideals, responses to engaging projects; no one would want to settle for small things. There are those who have the *gusto* of the Gospel and the fragrance of Heaven. They are men who live in silence, the silence that is the secret embroidery of holiness. Unknown men who, like the Wayfarer of Emmaus, approach our lives — that daily and sometimes tiring groove in which we are immersed. Men who have learned to wait for other men "at the doorstep." Men who have lived with one foot "among the things up there" and another "among the things down here." As a well-known scholar put it:

> The mystics are the most impressive servants
> of humanity the world has ever seen.[4]

---

[3] Didache
[4] Harvey D. Egan, SJ, *An Anthology of Christian Mysticism*

Father Candido Amantini represents this condition in the highest degree: he testified, through the self-sacrificing offering of himself to others, the possibility of a fully authentic life, marked by the love of God: charity. The saints teach us that happiness does not come from the outside but from within; and if there is nothing inside, there will never be happiness!

In looking around at the world, one realizes that poor men are ever increasing, not of material poverty but of experience. They are men who are ungenerous and stingy, closed-off in their selfishness. They are men who are empty and depleted in their inner essence. They are unable to comprehend beauty and to involve themselves with history and the world. They cannot take off their masks, revealing who they really are! Sometimes we, too, look back for a moment and calculate what we have left behind and what we have earned! Those who love are willing to "waste themselves."

Father Candido taught me that the cry of the dying Jesus, a sign of the abyss of sorrow, is our cry. On our crosses, He is nailed with us. The pain of man and the pain of God meet and intermingle on the Cross. Beneath all the pain of this world, we know that there is the suffering Christ, alone, lost in the sea of man's suffering. There is no anguish, no pain in the world in which Christ has not taken part. He is one of us. There is none of our pain that is not at the same time Christ's pain. He has so entered the heart of human misery that there can be no *solitary* sorrow in the world. Our weeping is God's weeping; our suffering is God's Passion.

CHAPTER ONE

THE LIFE OF FR. CANDIDO AMANTINI

F ATHER CANDIDO Amantini was born in Bagnolo, a hamlet in the municipality of Santa Fiora in the province of Grosseto (Tuscany), on Jan. 31, 1914, to Giovanni Battista and Diolinda Fratini. His father was a blacksmith and also managed a salt and tobacco shop. He was baptized on Feb. 7 with the names Eraldo Ulisse Mauro. He received the Sacrament of Confirmation on September 8, 1920. He spent his early childhood in his hometown where he attended elementary school and received excellent grades. He also attended a music school and played in the village band. He served as an altar boy in the parish.

He encountered the Passionists during a mission they preached in Bagnolo. At the age of twelve, after having finished elementary school, he entered the Passionists' minor seminary in Nettuno (Rome) on October 26, 1926. He remained there for three years until 1929, attending middle school.

On October 9, 1929, at the St. Joseph Retreat on Monte Argentario, he began his year of novitiate. His novice master was Venerable Nazareno Santolini. On the 23rd of the same month, he received the religious habit and was given the name Candido of the Immaculate Conception. On October 24, 1930, he made his profession of temporary vows. He was then transferred to the convent of Tavernuzze near Florence to complete his high school studies until 1932. He then moved to the community of Vinchiana-Ponte a Moriano (Lucca) to complete his studies of Philosophy and Theology. On January 31, 1933, he made his perpetual vows.

In 1936, he arrived in Rome, at the Holy Stairs, to earn his licentiate in theology at the Pontifical University of St. Thomas, known as the "Angelicum." He was ordained a priest on March 13, 1937. In 1938, he attended the Pontifical Biblical Institute and simultaneously taught Sacred Scripture in the seminary in Tavernuzze. He obtained a licentiate in Sacred Scripture in 1944.

Gifted with a great capacity for learning and an excellent knowledge of Greek, he also learned Hebrew, German, and Sanskrit. From 1941 to 1945 he taught Hebrew and Sacred Scripture to students in Vinchiano (Lucca) and Cura di Vetralla (Viterbo). From 1945 to 1947, he returned to the Scala Santa in Rome to teach seminarians. He was a highly regarded and sought-after teacher such that, from 1947 to 1960, he was transferred to the convent of Sts. John and Paul to teach at the Passionists' International Study Center also in Rome. In May 1961, his health failed, as a result of which he had to stop teaching and undergo a long hospitalization. He eventually recovered, but his activities changed completely.

The ministry of exorcism

While he was still a teacher, he occasionally worked alongside his confrere, Father Alessandro Coletti, who was an exorcist in the diocese of Arezzo. Father Candido then began performing his first exorcisms under the guidance of Father Alessandro. It was during this time that his first contacts with the man who would become St. Pio of Pietrelcina also began. From 1961 until his death in 1992,

Amantini stayed in the Holy Stairs community, ministering as an exorcist.

He combined deep doctrine to those charisms with which the Lord had enriched him abundantly. He had a special gift in understanding people and what they needed. Often, with his prayers and gift of spiritual seeing, he helped those who went to him even in dire material situations. His word, quiet and sure, was eagerly awaited.

He had a custom of getting up in the middle of the night to go to the chapel and pray an hour of Eucharistic Adoration. The faithful would flock to attend his morning Mass. In 1986, at the insistence of Cardinal Ugo Poletti, Father Gabriele Amorth placed himself under the training of Father Candido to learn and practice the ministry of exorcism.

The final years

In the final years of his life, his health increasingly deteriorated, and he was frequently hospitalized. At night, he was often assailed by fits of feeling suffocated and oppression of his heart. He felt death was near and spoke of it with serenity. He spent long periods of time immersed in prayer and absent from everything. In full consciousness, he received viaticum from his confessor, Father Benigno, on the night of Sept. 22, 1992. That night, assisted by some confreres, still perfectly lucid, he died saintly in his room in the retreat of the Pontifical Sanctuary of the Holy Stairs, singing, "You come down from the stars [...]," [1] and often repeating the scriptural verse, "O how much it cost you to have loved us."

On March 21, 2012, his mortal remains were moved from the Verano Monumental Cemetery to the Chapel of the Crucifix within the Pontifical Sanctuary of the Holy Stairs in Rome. In order to investigate his actual practice of Christian virtues to a heroic degree, on July 13, 2012, the Passionist

---

[1] Likely the famous Italian Christmas carol, "Tu scendi dalle stelle," originally written by St. Alphonsus Liguori. – Ed.

Congregation at the Vicariate of Rome officially opened the Diocesan Inquiry into the life, virtues, and reputation for holiness of the Servant of God, Candido Amantini. It was happily concluded on November 16, 2016.

CHAPTER TWO

THE PATIENCE OF LISTENING

A life of contemplation

HE SOUL OF Father Amantini's work was established on the contemplative dimension of life, which he always lived in deep communion with the Lord Jesus, nourishing it through Eucharistic Adoration. One certainty animated, indeed *inflamed*, his heart: Jesus present in the Eucharist; and it was precisely this certainty that made him an instrument of mercy.

Father Candido, therefore, always shone for his great piety and priestly charity. He was an apostle of mercy. Moved by the inner piety that inflamed his heart, he poured out all his strength for the conversion of those far away. God was always the goal of his thoughts, and he worked everything for Him and in Him. He spent himself toward this end.

Sincere humility, long-suffering patience, affable meekness, discreet prudence: he could be said to have fully implemented St. Paul's invitation to Titus: *In omnibus praebe teipsum exemplum bonorum operum* ("show yourself in all respects a model of good deeds") (Titus 2:7) presenting in himself, thus, the model of the perfect priest.

His heart palpitated for all that was worthy of commiseration. Those who resorted to him under the weight of misfortune descended the steps of the Pontifical Sanctuary of the Holy Stairs with a ray of light on their faces and a singular peace in their souls.

He was humble, silent, hidden, patient in listening to people, able to bestow God's mercy. Many affirm, even today, that he was able to read hearts, to understand the torments of others simply by looking into their eyes. Tender, patient, and merciful with everyone; in approaching him, one had the impression of being directly in touch with God, such was the joy and serenity he conveyed.

The "occupation of the confessional"

He wiped away the warm tears that streaked down the faces of the melancholy, of those who had lost their joy: his fundamental occupation was always the confessional; we might say that he was an apostle of it, on par with the great confessors such as Father Mandic, Father Cappello, Father Cafasso, and others.

When he was requested to hear confessions, he did not mind the inconvenience or fatigue. And his love for the Lord could be measured precisely by those energies he poured out in the confessional. There in that "tribunal of mercy" one could see his gracefulness and charity toward his neighbor in listening to sins and counseling, most often limiting himself to quoting a phrase from Holy Scripture or a thought of the holy founding father of the Passionists, Paul of the Cross. All kinds of people went to him. He had this gift, moreover: with just a few words, he removed all scruples and calmed souls. Many of his penitents still remember that in giving absolution he was transfigured. They still remember his calm, serene, and smiling face, never impatient or upset while giving absolution or while blessing.

A blessing: this was, in fact, Father Candido Amantini, "the exorcist of Rome," a blessing on the world. His life, more precisely, was the blessing of God on the world. A long blessing suspended, in eternity, between Heaven and Earth. A blessing for me! — for all of us. He blesses me, such as I am, with my many bitternesses and thousand poverties. He blesses me with my many doubts and labors. He blesses! — a blessing that enters the depths of all lives, of my life.

Thus it was that, before that blessing hand, those far from God returned to Him: the sick were healed, the wayward found the right path, solutions were brought out for impossible problems, and unclean spirits were cast out. Boundless throngs of souls went to receive that blessing, to receive counsel, to confess, to attend "his" Mass. His blessing was, in truth, Jesus Christ, the "blessing par excellence," whereby, in quoting St. Paul, "We have been blessed by God in Christ." (Eph. 1:3)

Amantini was aware that no soul is easily won over. It takes time. Patience. The enemy, Satan, does not abandon him so easily, because he knows that every soul won to Christ, hastens for him his ultimate defeat. For Satan, one might say, it is a matter of survival to draw souls into his net. That is why Father Candido was the man who radiated God, because he had only one torment, the torment of saving man, and to save him at any cost.

CHAPTER THREE

A REFLECTION OF GOD'S LOVE

Through the Saints, God reaches the heart of man

I HAVE ALWAYS thought that the Lord is a thief, though a very strange thief. He is one who steals nothing, gives everything, and comes away with his hands perpetually full. One who does not tire of giving. And He gives us all of Himself in an overflowing measure. One who keeps offering Himself to His Church.

There are men and women in our lives through whom God warms the heart; through whom God reaches the heart of man. Theologian Hans Urs von Balthasar wrote that the saints

> are the most important commentary on the Gospel [...] they are the incarnation of the incarnate Word of God and therefore truly a gateway to Jesus.

In their biographies, they are not closed-off in historical data; instead, they reveal an evangelical "lesson." They are unique, special, and particular. They are for me, today. The saints

are not to be imitated pedestrianly, but in
doing, as they did, the will of God. [...] We
must live out our holiness today, keeping in
mind that it must bloom in the flower-bed of
the Church where here are already a thousand
fragrances. (Chiara Lubich)

The world, and even the Church, still needs Jesus Christ
— and His faith; His strong message of radicality; His Cross,
death and resurrection; and His most precious Blood. The
world, and its people, does not need merely to resolve the
problems of their daily lives, to feel at peace with themselves
regardless of their shortcomings, without any kind of
judgment, without any kind of morality, without any kind of
faith that demands a path of conversion and, consequently,
the imposition of a change of choices and perspectives, which
presuppose a change of life.

The world still needs Jesus: the real one, the one of the
Gospel, the one who says He is *the Way, the Truth, and the Life.*
The saints are "as the colors of the spectrum in relation to
light." Further,

their very diversity is a living tribute to their
unique richness, which they compose like the
colors of the rainbow. The lives of the saints
are like a catechism in images, an illustration
of the values of life contained in the one
Gospel.

That is why, in reading their biographies and meditating
on their examples — just as one meditates on the verses of
the Gospel — they can offer new stimuli and new abilities to
build a world that is a little more human because it is more
immersed in the divine. Father Candido, like so many
Christians still today, thankfully, kept alive that *love filled
with wonder* that is the departure point of an authentically
human existence; a wonder that is found, for example, already

16

alive in the gaze of the child who opens his eyes for the first time and sees his mother's smile.

This is because only love, dare I say *true love*, is credible, because the one who loves is credible. A love that offers everything, that strips itself of everything: like Jesus, credible because He stripped Himself of everything, refusing to "keep anything for Himself." Amantini is a credible man. That is why he still captivates today: he triumphs. Although many did not know him in life — not even I, who am writing, and I regret it — everyone, however, before his grave feels a longing for God, proposes to live a better life; he arrives troubled, melancholic, in despair, and goes away serene and with the spirit to return. Amantini was a man of deep penance. His life was a "bombardment" of love. He affected everyone, even those far away. He also affected me, I can affirm. The "bomb went off," and its shockwave hit everyone inevitably, everyone indiscriminately.

God's love opens the ways of knowledge

Amantini was a man in love with God. The love of God, in fact, filtered through the lives of the saints, launches its greatest provocation to men — even to us: in love, the ways of knowledge are opened. Love alone creates a future and sets us free; Love always remains before us as an unexplored frontier full of possibilities. Faith is risk; it entails, however, a margin of healthy insecurity.

Father Candido recognized in his life that he was loved: this is why everything became a sign of that love that constituted his existence. He lived with an attitude that desires and seeks the sign of God in everything, which is then the common denominator of any path to holiness. Unfortunately, the

> psychology of the tomb is developing, which little by little turns Christians into museum mummies. Disappointed by reality, by the

Church, or by themselves, they experience the constant temptation to cling to a hopeless, sweetish sadness that takes hold of the heart like "the most precious of the devil's elixirs." (Georges Bernanos)

I was reading this thought in a booklet by Jean-Paul Hernández:

What a child learning to walk must overcome when he or she takes that first step is fear. Fear of falling and getting hurt. At the root, it is fear of dying. (*This is what makes the faith difficult.*)

Father Candido's life was lived the only way it should have been lived, in the only way it could be handed back to the Father: at the foot of the Cross. The word "Gospel" means "good news": Amantini was the daily Gospel to so many smaller souls, more oppressed (by evil), and who found in Him a proclamation of deliverance and peace. He was the sycamore on which we all climbed to see Jesus; to cross, if only for a moment, His gaze of love and deliverance. In this regard, the words of Benedict XVI are profoundly true. He notes that

The lives of the saints are not limited to their earthly biographies but also include their being and working in God after death. In the saints one thing becomes clear: those who draw near to God do not withdraw from men, but rather become truly close to them. (*Deus caritas est*, 42)

Man is by no means created to be caged inside the narrow spaces of a comfortable, quiet life full of every consumer commodity! Sin continues to invite one to lower one's gaze, downsize one's horizons, or settle for a life that is not even a semblance of what man is called to be. In listening to those whose spiritual director was the Servant of God, what commonly emerges is an attempt on the part of the revered priest to direct souls toward God by helping them avoid being "shaped by downward temptation."

Sometimes it may happen that we reject a testimony or a life that carries within it a seed of Life and infinity. Sometimes it can happen that we reject a witness of holiness who appears to us as "too high"; many choose, in fact, to remain firmly upon the earth because it is more comfortable and without too much risk. But can a man who loves ever give up the pursuit of the Beloved? No, absolutely not.

To disentangle ourselves today from the many proposals which life offers to us is not easy. Father Candido invites us to rediscover the law of the seed, the Cross, and the absolute awareness that only in the total offering of ourselves is our vocation fully realized.

The essential qualities that live within Father Candido

I believe, without exaggerating, that the entire panorama of the spiritual life unfolds before our eyes through some essential qualities that begin with the experience of our Servant of God:

- devotion to Mary Most Holy.
- adherence to the Roman Pontiff.
- *knowledge of suffering.*
- hope of future good.
- commitment to reaching the heights of Christian perfection.

Cherishing his life, Amantini was vibrant with the mission to walk the path of the Gospel with simplicity and love. His casual simplicity recalls the values of the Gospel. His total death to self, his delicate ecclesial service, his surrender to the Lord's will, his prompt and serene obedience, fueled by the power of prayer, make this humble Passionist priest a model of incarnate holiness, a strong and incisive witness.

Christocentric spirituality and the Heart of Jesus

The spirituality of our Servant of God is a Christocentric spirituality, an incarnational spirituality that made him take on the most delicate sentiments of the Heart of Jesus. This was probably the secret, left to us as a testament, of his vigorous theological life. It gave his personality a wholly unique imprint, helping him to unleash all his human and spiritual resources, in the apostolic commitment to conquer souls to Christ and in the struggle against evil.

His life testimony, imbued with the Gospel, unmasks and "puts to flight" the dark machinations of that pharisaic bourgeoisie that sometimes infects even us, when works don't match words or the *"Truth of Life."* We need to flee from the lethargy of a zero-cost Christian life: just as did our Servant of God.

The greatest risk, at times, is to be without dreams and to be so conformed to the world that we lose the salt of life, that which gives flavor, that which gives meaning, enthusiasm to our living, to our struggling and suffering. There are men who grasp life tightly and spend their time focused on themselves — "navel-gazing." Father Candido reminds us, instead, that against all logic, the only secret to happiness is to give up everything for Jesus of Nazareth and the Gospel: to lose possessions, power, or success in order to open ourselves to the surprise of being a gift for those around us, a universal gift.

A life without God is truly a succession of lost hours. By attaining the *heights of holiness,* Father Candido taught us to renounce a life of wasted hours, avoiding locking ourselves up in the steel cages of narrow-minded thinking!

If, in spite of everything, we remain closed to His voice, preferring our own securities, disguised even by rituals, prayers, etc., and risk creating and enclosing ourselves in a muffled, perhaps even flashy, world, we will be alone because that very world will not be inhabited by God.

God is like the crevices in the rock — a tender, motherly refuge that always welcomes us, protecting us gently. This is enough for us!

CHAPTER FOUR

THE MAN WHO LOOKED PAIN IN THE FACE

Exorcism and the Eucharist: the same frame of mind

FATHER CANDIDO was asked one day during an interview, "Do you feel lonely? What is in your soul when you exorcise?" The Servant of God answered, quite naturally:

> It is like when I celebrate Mass, although they are two different things. The inner disposition is the same: I am carrying out a ministry related not to my person, but to my priesthood; related to Jesus' command to "Cast out demons." It is an action of the Church, which is the Church Militant.

Father Giorgio Alessandri, years later, still remembers the large crowd of faithful who waited each day to be received by Amantini:

> As a boy, when I was about 13 or 14 years old, especially in the summertime when school was out, I would go to the Holy Stairs very early and see, outside the gate, an endless line of

people waiting for the Holy Stairs to open. I would ask, "But who's there? For whom are you waiting?" They would answer, "We wish…we must talk to Father Candido." "Who is Father Candido?" I would ask. [...] Sometimes people would arrive before 3:00 a.m.; a long line would form in front of the large gate of the Holy Stairs, so then people would stop for the celebration of Holy Mass.

Father Candido attracted so many people precisely because of such personable traits. His life of great fidelity, of such great constancy in humility, and moreover imbued with daily toil in discerning what was wisest, most opportune, but also most generous and most in accordance with the will of God, won over those who came to him. For this reason, even in his lifetime, he was held in high esteem and good reputation both by religious and by all the faithful. He fulfilled his ministerial duties and the Rule of the Passionist Congregation in an excellent manner. He was totally a man of God. He was always united to prayer. He always carried the rosary in his hand, as he understood well that the rosary fills with vitality the souls who know how to make it their own, in recitation,

> the joy of the messianic times, the salvific suffering of Christ and the glory of the Risen Lord which fills the Church. (*Marialis cultus*, 49a)

…and he was very devoted, as will be presented, to the Blessed Virgin.

Inner coherence, in every ministry

The promotion of the Cause for canonization of our Servant of God, besides continuing to concretize the teaching of the Second Vatican Council on the universal call to holiness, constitutes, moreover, a reminder of the beauty of the religious and priestly vocation. Those who knew Amantini, attracted by the appeal of his devotion to God, attested to his profound coherence among being and acting, among the happiness and fidelity in living in the following of the chaste, poor, and obedient Christ, to his desire, ever alive, to distance himself from all forms of superficiality and appearance. What Blessed Teresa Mary of the Cross (1846-1910), foundress of the Carmelite Sisters of Saint Teresa, says of the saints can be said of Father Candido:

> Saints are not made with a brush, but with a
> chisel: on Mt. Tabor they are sketched, while
> on Mt. Calvary they are perfected.

Father Candido, in fact, was a man of God: loved by God. He loves and lived by love, in perfect harmony with the new commandment left to us by Christ, namely that of loving one another as He has loved us.[1] This explains his intense faith life; it also explains his intense life of piety and prayer; a life sustained by the Eucharistic Celebration and direct contact with the Word. A disciple of the Crucified, he embodied the spirituality of the *Christus patiens* (Suffering Christ). This profound spirituality is expressed in the classic *Imitation of Christ*:

> Jesus has always many who love His heavenly
> kingdom, but few who bear His cross. He has
> many who desire consolation, but few who
> care for trial. He finds many to share His table,
> but few to take part in His fasting. All desire
> to be happy with Him; few wish to suffer
> anything for Him. Many follow Him to the
> breaking of bread, but few to the drinking of
> the chalice of His passion. Many revere His

---

[1] See John 13:34–35.

miracles; few approach the shame of the Cross. Many love Him as long as they encounter no hardship; many praise and bless Him as long as they receive some comfort from Him. But if Jesus hides Himself and leaves them for a while, they fall either into complaints or into deep dejection. Those, on the contrary, who love Him for His own sake and not for any comfort of their own, bless Him in all trial and anguish of heart as well as in the bliss of consolation. Even if He should never give them consolation, yet they would continue to praise Him and wish always to give Him thanks.

Following the Crucifix

"Following the Crucifix" explains the life of the Servant of God. Hearer, narrator, and guardian of the Word, Father Candido listened and allowed himself to be guided by the Gospel: he seized all opportunities to proclaim God's love and mercy. He became, thus, a man of balance and harmony. Balance and harmony between "the things of Heaven" and "those of the Earth." Here I like to recall a thought of the novelist Mario Pomilio, who writes in his work, *The Fifth Gospel*:

> Holiness is a plant that has its crown in Heaven and its roots in the desert.

Balance, we said, according to the apostle Paul's exhortation:

> If then you have been raised with Christ, seek the things that are above, where Christ is, seated at the right hand of God. Set your minds on things that are above, not on things that are on earth. (Col. 3:1-2)

He was a careful guardian of the things of God and the things of man: a supportive friend of the poor, of the sick (in body and spirit), and of the needy and marginalized. He was always available and discreet, often on tiptoe. He was a priest in deep harmony with the Magisterium: within the Church and with the Church. He was what the theologian Henri De Lubac would say about him in the Council years about the man of the Church and his characteristics:

> The Church has stolen his heart. She is his spiritual homeland. [...] She is his mother and his brothers. Nothing that regards her leaves him indifferent or insensitive. He takes root in her, is formed in her image, becomes part of her experience, and feels rich in her riches. He has the consciousness of participating through her and her alone, in the stability of God. From the Church, he learns how to live and die. He does not judge her but allows himself to be judged by her. He joyfully accepts to sacrifice everything to her unity. (*Meditations on the Church*)

Father Candido never forgets that he is a man: his daily life is made up of waiting and encountering, welcoming and listening, compassion and solidarity, sharing and service; with humility and discretion, trust and patience. In his universal embrace, a privileged place occupies moral and spiritual poverties. He hurries to meet everyone to fill inner voids, discomforts, and anxieties; he breaks himself as the Bread, to help his brother or sister in the search to rediscover the light of a hope for life. Someone recalls that:

> Even during vacations in the village, he always made himself available to the sick and suffering. People came to him from afar — those who already frequented him in Rome, to

receive his blessings. His word, even his mere presence, was a consolation. He would dedicate himself to others, help and comfort, to the utmost of his strength.

Not shirking the pain

He carried out intense activity alongside those most in need, even when his own condition was far from good. Father Candido embodied the pain of man even physically, like many mystics of the twentieth century. Father Alfredo Pallotta, who was his student and who followed in his footsteps in the ministry of exorcist, thus remembers him:

> It made an impression on us young people to contemplate his gaunt face, especially with his nickname that the cook, Brother John, had given him (it was his custom to do so with everyone); he had branded him with the title *"Cristo Spirante."* (i.e. "Christ expiring")

Amantini did not shy away from pain: he accepted and welcomed it. He entered into the mystery of the human condition. Father Candido "collaborated" with God so that he could cultivate in man, in any man, that true, authentic, and mature humanity that is the authentic reflection of the divine light in the world, which is thus, the theological place of God in the world, the place where the action of the Spirit makes us recover the unity between human and spiritual, between self-knowledge and knowledge of God. In God, the human person becomes himself and takes on the mission of making history human, of sharing with creation the freedom to which it aspires, giving it a fully human meaning. The French philosopher Emmanuel Mounier notes:

> I really do not want to say anything to you because the pain is so great that to describe it

with words becomes unbearable. Pain does not have a face, it does not have a certain name, and, nonetheless, you will see that pain is the most tangible of faces, it is the most steadfast of friends, and it is the most fruitful of our works. [...] Leave open to him not only the words of remembering but also the words of presence and hope. [...] It is necessary to suffer so that truth does not crystallize into doctrine but is born of the flesh. (*Letters on Pain: A Look at the Mystery of Suffering*)

It is worthwhile, then, to remind ourselves that even in sorrow God is not an empty word, a distant story, but an eternal account of love that came to tell itself in time — ours, so that each person, by listening and believing, may be reached and transformed by Him, in Him.

Some time ago, not long ago from the present era, in a time of sorrow, a little Jewish girl named Anne Frank wrote:

It is a great miracle that I have not given up all my hopes because they seem absurd and unachievable. I keep them still, in spite of everything, because I still believe that people are really good at heart. I simply cannot build up my hopes on a foundation consisting of confusion, misery, and death. I see the world gradually being turned into a wilderness, I hear the ever-approaching thunder, which will destroy us too, I can feel the sufferings of millions and yet, if I look up into the heavens, I think that it will all come right, that this cruelty too will end, and that peace and tranquility will return again.

Behold, this is what Father Candido — "the exorcist of Rome" — did; he helped many not to give up hope, not to abandon themselves to despair. He sustained many men and women to know how to hope that God would never give up His purpose for humanity, teaching that the Christian faith does not exempt man from living, all the way, "inside" our many fearful situations. In the journey of faith, we will notice people walking at different speeds and in different ways. There will be those who walk faster and those who walk slower; there will be those who fall and those who get back on their feet and resume the journey; there will be those who then arrive more quickly by demonstrating heroic virtues.

Father Candido taught us that God cares nothing about where man may be: near or far, at home or lost, behind the bars of a prison or free — in the monotony of the dull ordinary life. His Paternal heart will always be there, beating like a lover waiting for a sign, a word. We have exiled Him from life and history, from our pain and our joys, from our daily life and our journey. Yet, He does not cease to become, with us, struggle and hope.

CHAPTER FIVE

CONFRONTING EVIL!

Shining stars

HOLINESS COMES from an intimate relationship with the One whom Scripture calls "Thrice holy."
Today, as Elio Guerriero puts it:

> By increasing beatifications and canonizations, Pope John Paul II led territorial ecclesial communities to pay more attention to their saints, to cultivate remembrance through study and devotion. [...] In their company then we can go with Jesus to a place set apart, so as to penetrate deeper into revelation. (*I Santi della Bibbia*) (*The Saints of the Bible*)

The figure of the Servant of God, Father Candido — whom these pages wish to celebrate — fascinates and enlightens. His experience of faith convinces that holiness is a proposal for everyone. Truly. He deeply loved Christ and his Church.

This figure persuades us to consider that God, in every age, raises up men and women on whom He bestows very special graces, making them living witnesses of His unchanging love. They drag us along with their lives, and we cannot help but look up to them with admiration. The saints are like shining stars in a world full of confusion and disorder.

Some of those who knew him in person recall an incident that they often told me and which I summarize as follows:

> One day a lady came to Father asking for a blessing for a small crucifix of hers. So she opened her hands and revealed a little chain, the kind worn around the neck, with a gold cross. Father Candido was ready to impart the blessing when suddenly he stopped and stiffened. Father Amorth, who was present, noticed that somewhat hidden by the woman's hand, there was a cornet, also made of gold and also attached to the chain.[1] Father Candido's face darkened. His meek voice rose sternly in the church, with an authority that no one had ever heard: "You do not realize what you are doing. You cannot confuse Christ with these things. Just go away. Throw everything away. And come back only when you have chosen between Jesus and the devil."

This helps us understand how in the heart of the Servant of God burned a living flame of charity for the Truth and for God that literally consumed him and favored him with sublime favors. His Christian life was built on a most solid foundation: the tabernacle, the Word of God, God's will, Marian devotion, and the sacraments. His life was one of prayer and ministry, and he knew well how to distinguish between God's presence and magic.

---

[1] The Neapolitan *corno* or *cornetto*, in the shape of a red, twisted horn, is an amulet or charm superstitiously believed to ward off the evil eye. -Ed.

Father Candido reminds us that today's Church needs saints everywhere, not only in convents or before the altars, but in families, workplaces, and all areas of human activity. The saints have accepted the world and have become an authentic hope for the world. They are not afraid to surrender to God, to leave their securities, or to set foot in deserted places! They took the risk of getting their hands dirty with the lives of others.

Georges Saint-Bonnet's definition in this regard is felicitous:

> A saint is, first and foremost, an extraordinary man or woman in whom God dwells, but he is also a response to the spiritual needs of a generation; and the saint is a man or woman who is an eminent illustration of the ideas that Christians of old had of holiness.

The ministry of the exorcist

The ministry of the exorcist is a "most delicate" one that cannot be practiced superficially or half-heartedly. Exorcism is a struggle, sometimes a very difficult one, against the power of Satan; it is a struggle that demands union with the Cross of Christ, humility, vigilance, prudence, purity, courage, and trust in the power of God's love — all corroborated by great patience and a living faith.

Today, the need for religion has not disappeared in modern man, but the contemporary request takes on different connotations — ones that are deeper and existential, more universal and experiential. Father Candido was deeply convinced of the need for absolute truth and the sharing of Christian values through an intense Christian life.

His homilies were imbued with concrete answers to keep the many souls from losing sight of those true values of life and faith. His pastoral effectiveness depended on his ability to question himself, the openness of his heart to sincere searching, and the courage to follow new paths. Father Candido, nevertheless, confronted secularism, the myths of success and money, religious relativism, and the subjectivism of faith with a tough attitude. He had strong words, and his meek character yielded when faced with all this.

Contemporary man, as we know, is immersed in a profoundly secularized world. Man risks becoming, thus, easy prey to a practical atheism and materialism preoccupied to the point of obsession with material well-being without any reference to spiritual values. Amantini understood this well, like the prophet he was, and he did everything he could to ensure that the desire for the Kingdom of God would sprout again in so many hearts. He understood that the violation of the sacred is another of the dark threats that await those who venture out into the unknown, but enticing, territories of discovery; that the revelation of what does not belong to our culture is often mysterious and risky. In this society of ours, day after day, we are witnessing a decrease in faith, and an increase in questions — and they are truly numerous — of those who request help in overcoming the (alleged) vexations or possession of the devil.

Dr. Valter Cascioli, a psychiatrist and spokesman for the International Association of Exorcists, said that "requests for exorcism have increased significantly." More and more people, precisely in this regard, are turning to esoteric or occult practices, even among believers. Yet, Scripture speaks quite clearly:

> There shall not be found among you any one who burns his son or his daughter as an offering, any one who practices divination, a soothsayer, or an augur, or a sorcerer, or a charmer, or a medium, or a wizard, or a necromancer. For whoever does these things is an abomination to the Lord. (Deut. 18:10-11)

Often, those who approach these practices feel as if they have the world at their command, but then suddenly find themselves alone, with their hands tied and deeply wounded.

The devil exists, and he struggles against us — all too often through devious or glamorously cloaked paths, sometimes violently, distressingly, and dramatically. Evil, in fact, as Cardinal Mauro Piacenza noted:

> is made particularly visible and, therefore, identifiable in the ministry of the exorcist priest, when, especially in the case of possession, the devil, by manifesting himself, shows his deliberate and intractable will to kill and possess, to deceive and usurp, to humiliate and offend.

Where there is evil, the evil one is always there. In a lecture, Father Candido spoke about the devil:

> In him, there is nothing left of light and good. So if one can say that God is the supreme good, then the devil is the supreme evil; he is the very personification of evil; there is no evil that does not depend on him. (Servant of God Lecture, Postulation Archives)

Against the "peddling" of evil

"Satan does what drug peddlers do in Scampia: in order to get hold of the customer, he offers the drugs at first for free," Father Pasquale Puca, a Jesuit and exorcist for the Archdiocese of Naples, stated in an interview (June 2011).

To this peddling of evil, hatred, and violence, Amantini's prayer was (and is) without a shadow of a doubt a great remedy, a strong dam that prevented and still prevents man from becoming habituated to evil, and especially to violence — which nourishes evil, and makes it grow to the point of negating others. In that same conference, Father Candido declared that:

> The Lord came into this world to eradicate the power of Satan; He gave His Church the power to eradicate the power of Hell in many ways; first of all, through Himself and by His death on the Cross. He therefore came to exorcise the devil, to cast him out. (He was the) first exorcist, we might say.

Servant of God Amantini knew well how to discern the different cases of possession, drawing from what is stated in the *Rite of Exorcism*, namely, behaviors such as: speaking fluently in unknown languages or understanding others speaking such languages, knowing distant or hidden knowledge, or demonstrating strengths beyond one's age or natural condition.

But, first of all, he certainly believed that the most significant sign was the manifestation of an overbearing and deep aversion to the sacred. In fact, the new *Rite of Exorcism* states the following in No. 16 of the General Premises:

> Therefore, it is also necessary to pay attention to other signs, especially of a moral and spiritual order, which reveal, in different forms, diabolic intervention. They may be a strong aversion to God, to the Most Holy Person of Jesus, to the Blessed Virgin Mary, to the Saints, to the Church, to the Word of God, to sacred realities, especially the sacraments, to sacred images.

Always with prudence

In any case, even in the face of certain manifestations that might have seemed obvious, Father Candido always evaluated each case with extreme caution and prudence. Sometimes there were things that were absolutely and humanly impossible based on the abilities of that particular person or in the expressions of his or her personality. This episode that I report below can help us better understand what has been written so far:

> One day, Father Candido was exorcising a strong woman who frequently went into rages. A psychiatrist was also present. At a certain point, the woman rose from her chair and spun around, as discus throwers do to increase momentum at the beginning of the throw, and, with her fist, unleashed with all her might a blow that struck the exorcist in the right temple. The noise of the punch reverberated in the spacious sacristy, and the doctor rushed over worriedly. But Father Candido continued his exorcism undaunted, with a smiling face, as was his custom. Later, he said that he felt as if a velvet glove had lightly grazed his temple. Evidently he had been protected by Heaven and, I do not hesitate to say, in an extraordinary way.

Amantini himself wrote in the preface to the book *An Exorcist Tells His Story*, written by his disciple Father Amorth:

> If, however, God allows some people to experience diabolical vexation, He has nevertheless provided them with powerful aids of various kinds. He has equipped the Church with very efficacious sacramental powers for this need. But also, against this nefarious activity of Satan, God has elected the Blessed Virgin as a permanent antidote, because of that

enmity He sanctioned from the beginning between the two adversaries.

He had direct experience, in fact, of the commendable power of intercession conferred on Mary Most Holy in the struggle against the devil, first of all by virtue of her immaculacy, as Father Candido himself notes in his treatise on Mariology, to which we will refer later, *The Mystery of Mary.* This is a power that comports a most complete victory over Satan, inasmuch as Mary has never been touched by the clutches of the devil! She is the Woman who personally crushes the head of the serpent.

For this reason, a life without Christ is like a tomb where one dwells in the worst slavery. A life without Christ is perpetually in the grip of a violent force that binds man and enslaves him.

You cannot tame evil

Yesterday, as today, we try to domesticate evil, forgetting its author and thus making ourselves even more enslaved by it:

> All forms of divination are to be rejected: recourse to Satan or demons, conjuring up the dead or other practices falsely supposed to "unveil" the future. Consulting horoscopes, astrology, palm reading, interpretation of omens and lots, the phenomena of clairvoyance, and recourse to mediums all conceal a desire for power over time, history, and, in the last analysis, other human beings, as well as a wish to conciliate hidden powers. They contradict the honor, respect, and loving fear that we owe to God alone. (*Catechism of the Catholic Church,* 2011)

Our virtual world has swallowed the real world, practically creating a parallel world, where it is believed that the same laws do not apply to us as our own do. But no one, in any world, can think of taming evil, which, instead, always turns against those who procure it, because evil always has something masochistic about it.

Father Gabriele Amorth recalled, again, an episode:

One day a priest was helping Father Candido. A young man was being exorcised when his clothes caught fire at one point. It was nothing serious, just a slight burn on one shoulder. His mother later said that his t-shirt touching the skin was also burned, but no harm was done to the young man. An acrid smell of sulfur was released during the burn, and the demon turned to the assisting priest, promising that he would pay dearly for it. A few days later, that priest was driving from Naples to Rome in the evening. He saw lights to his side. As he did not understand what they were, he decided to stop at a gas station. As he was on his way there, the car caught fire. The priest managed to stop, take out the keys, and get out. Other drivers rushed over, shouting, "There's someone inside! We can see someone!" But the priest vainly assured that he was alone. Suddenly, from the burning car, they heard that the engine was being started, and the car began to move slowly, like a fireball, toward the gasoline pumps. At the same time, an acrid smell of sulfur was perceptible in the air. The priest recognized the same smell during the exorcism and began to pray. Immediately the car stopped, but it continued to burn until it was totally destroyed.

Father Candido, being the far-sighted man that he was, would certainly have suggested that we remain vigilant regarding practices that are rampant today especially among the young (and old), such as channeling, Ouija boards, spiritism, "enlightened masters," invisible spiritual friends, angel worship (God's angels are not to be worshipped; indeed their worship is strictly forbidden, see Col. 2:18),[2] automatic writing, séances, scrying bowls, telepathy, yoga, reiki and other practices derived from Eastern religions, radiesthesia, meditation, hypnosis, magnetism, group dynamism, New Age alternative medicine, and so on. It is best not to play with fire! Many of these "places" (let's refer to them as such) are unfamiliar and many are unknown and often taken for granted. They are "places" laden with mysterious and uncertain presences. Father Candido taught that human life is a continual search for water within the various negative experiences of cracked cisterns.

Given everything, we live in a time of great recovery of those pseudo-spiritual values: evidence of this can be seen in the expansive spread of techniques and customs from the Far East (yoga, reiki, etc.) or the great publishing success, all over the world, of texts about angels or demons and so on.

The "weight" of pain

Our inner questions lead us to believe that God has abandoned us in our suffering, pain, and despair. We wonder why God who is love and mercy has not protected us and answered our pleas. Too often we wonder why He does not help us now to overcome our pain: to heal it, to cure it. We feel abandoned: sometimes even by our loved ones. We are even more convinced that we have been left alone even by the

---

[2] This refers to an occult practice of invoking so-called "angels" and often treating them like gods, calling upon them in ways forbidden by the Church. The Church, however, in the proper manner, venerates and requests the assistance of the holy angels, who, as powerful spiritual creatures, have been assigned by God for our protection and for our aid in the pursuit of salvation. -Ed.

One who created us; by the One who loves us. The saints, on the other hand:

> For by reason of the fact that those in heaven are more closely united with Christ, they establish the whole Church more firmly in holiness, lend nobility to the worship which the Church offers to God here on earth and in many ways contribute to its greater edification. (cf. 1 Cor. 12:12-27) For after they have been received into their heavenly home and are present to the Lord (cf. 2 Cor. 5:8), through Him and with Him and in Him they do not cease to intercede with the Father for us, showing forth the merits which they won on earth through the one Mediator between God and man (cf. 1 Tim. 2:5), serving God in all things and filling up in their flesh those things which are lacking of the sufferings of Christ for His Body which is the Church. (cf. Col. 1:24). (*Lumen Gentium*, 49)

From the various and diverse testimonies about the Servant of God, some of which were gathered from the living voice of those who knew him while he was alive — and there are still many — I understood that Father Candido was clear that pain and despair have an enormous bearing on our relationship with God. The loss of hope foments our myriad doubts about His "ability" to help us, thus raising new and increasingly confusing questions about the meaning of our existence. Too often the pain, the various crosses that we bear in the silence of our nights, lead us to believe that we have been abandoned. It all makes us question God's faithfulness. It leads to the rejection of God, and then, to the rejection of ourselves. Unfortunately, today:

There is a sickness that hollows out the souls and hearts of so many people: they feel deeply lonely, unloved, empty, parched, closed, and imprisoned inside glass castles that are beautiful to look at but terrible to inhabit. (Father Paul Monaco, S.J.)

Father Candido was able to take up the cry for help, a desperate cry that other men could not or did not understand. The experience of our Servant of God teaches us that the Christian life never ceases to be the fruit of a conquest, of a strenuous journey of *disavowal* of the old man in us to make full room for the presence and action of the new man created by God.

For many years, Father Candido confronted evil: he fought it with the strength of his priestly ministry. This is why he knew how to keep hope alive, which is never a form of evasion from reality or, even worse, a rejection of it; rather, it is a form of participation and commitment within history to transform it according to the logic of the Kingdom.

Do you know why Father Candido is credible? Because he broke the screens and the restricted circles and the narrow views of our existence, to then open us to the horizons of a life as children of God.

One may ask again: is Father Candido's delicate ministry complete? Absolutely not. In fact, it continues through numerous exorcist priests, engaged in different countries of the world, who carry on zealously and arduously the work accomplished by our Servant of God, who revived and enhanced the service of mercy of the ministry of exorcism in the Church.

CHAPTER SIX

A LIFE IMBUED WITH GOD

Love, the common thread of Christian mysticism

I HAVE ALWAYS been captivated by the study of the Catholic mystics. While immersed, thus, in the normal everyday life, they always seem to be animated and guided by an intimate, transcendent light, which restores the correct proportions to everything else (even to the dramatic events of the world, of history, and of our lives); it is as if they have different keys, always new, to read and interpret the world that surrounds them. This is not to estrange themselves and detach themselves from history, but to discover effective and credible answers. In mysticism, everything begins with God; it is He who takes the initiative. It is He who opens the soul and guides it; it is always He who directs, strengthens, and sustains the soul. He alone is its constant nourishment and total and all-embracing joy. The common thread of the mystics, thus, is love. Love is the ubiquitous theme. They live with God by drawing on His endless love, which they naturally manifest and pour out on their neighbor in innumerable ways and in myriad activities.

God is an irrepressible inner fire for them (as for the prophet Jeremiah)[1], leading them to "burn" for Him. In the words of philosopher Henri Bergson:

> The love that consumes the mystic is no longer simply the love of one man toward God, it is the love of God for all men. Through God, with God, the mystic loves all humanity with a divine love.

This love does not impoverish or weaken, it does not deplete the mystic (the believer, anyway) of his talents, rather, it enriches him and gives another dimension to his being "man."

> The humanity of the mystics is as if it is empowered by the mystic's own encounter with Christ: through the experience of Christ, he further shapes his own human profile [...] The result is always that the personal encounter with the God-One in Jesus Christ does not diminish the personality but strengthens it. (Josef Sudbrack)

The mystique of Father Candido

Can we also speak of a mystical life regarding Father Candido?

Certainly — if we understand the mystical life according to what Francesco Asti, a Neapolitan priest and Consultor to the Congregation for the Causes of Saints, stated in his book *Teologia della vita mistica. Fondamenti, dinamiche, mezzi,* Libreria Editrice Vaticana (*Theology of the Mystical Life. Foundations, Dynamics, Means*). The mystical life is a

---

[1] "If I say, 'I will not mention Him, or speak any more in His name,' there is in my heart as it were a burning fire shut up in my bones, and I am weary with holding it in, and I cannot." (Jeremiah 20:9)

movement of communion with God, called precisely not only mystical, but *the* mystical life, as a journey of faith lived in daily life, as a baptismal development of God's gifts. In this perspective it is also understood that

> the mystical path [...] does not concern only the monk or nun who retreats to the desert, but every believer, in that the transforming encounter with God takes place when the soul is united with Him. (*ibid.*)

Amantini demonstrated that he clearly understood that deep communion with God is not a utopia, but an offered possibility that is blocked only by sin: hence the need for constant and severe mortification to adhere to his love. Giannino Piana notes moreover that:

> the mystical life is characterized by an awareness of the presence within oneself of the living God, the God of love. As such, it is not the result of effort, because man is incapable of accessing it by his own strength alone. It is a divine gift. But such a gift cannot be attained unless one marches swiftly and patiently on the difficult path of prayer; unless one is committed to fulfilling, faithfully, day by day, the will of God; unless one allows oneself to unveil (or acknowledge) one's profound misery and renounces definitively self-pleasure; above all, unless one obstinately believes in the Father's love, accepting the purifications of this love.

We are all called to this experience of mystical union with God; we cannot escape it. No one can fail to do so, precisely by virtue of the baptism received. This is also affirmed (and confirmed) by the Catechism of the Catholic Church:

> Spiritual progress tends toward ever more intimate union with Christ. This union is called "mystical" because it participates in the mystery of Christ through the sacraments – "the holy mysteries" – and, in him, in the mystery of the Holy Trinity. God calls us all to this intimate union with him, even if the special graces or extraordinary signs of this mystical life are granted only to some for the sake of manifesting the gratuitous gift given to all.[2]

If we wanted to write about extraordinary signs, various anecdotes, or cases of exorcisms or healings, there would be much to say. Rosina, the elder sister of the Servant of God, recalls a case that Father Candido himself told her one day:

> Once, he was riding in a car together with Fr. Orlando[3]; perhaps there was something wrong with the car because, at a certain point, they heard a strange noise. They considered taking it to the mechanic's shop to have it checked out. The road they were driving on was uphill. All of a sudden, the car stopped and they could not get it going again. So they left it where it stopped and, walking slowly, they arrived on foot to an automotive garage. As they were considering how to get it towed, they saw to their amazement and surprise that their car was moving; it drove itself directly in front of them and stopped at the garage. The

---

[2] CCC 2014
[3] A priest-friend of Fr. Amantini.

mechanics found nothing wrong at all, so they quietly set off again.

And another,

> Once, while he was walking down the corridor, suddenly a rather young Passionist priest came up to Father Candido. With a mocking air, he looked at him and said, "Please stop with these imaginary evils of yours." Father Candido did not answer him, but he remained displeased, because he endured many evils. Days passed. All of a sudden, he saw that young Passionist again who was coming to him to greet him. Father Candido told him that what he had said had greatly offended him. But that confrere was so astonished, claiming that he had not done so. In fact, other Passionists intervened and affirmed that he had been away from Rome in those days. Then Father Candido understood that it had been the devil.

These episodes in the life of our Servant of God remind us that faith is an act of love. It is a trusting surrender, a perpetual living in God and of God. Because Love, the real kind, changes the way we see. From this I have often wondered how much we would gain in the Christian life if the ardent yearning for holiness were to neutralize and replace that *aurea mediocritas* (golden mediocrity) that makes the soul relax, too often, in half-measures and in so many small compromises. Such a recovery of vitality would bring to our evangelization, to our faith, to our being *Church*, to our being believable and credible witnesses, and to our belonging to Christ, the burning longing for holiness.

I have always been moved, on the other hand, in concluding this reflection, by another detail of the life of our

Servant of God. A spiritual daughter of his recalls a moment shared with Father Candido, who, with a moved voice and shining eyes, confided to her:

> I must tell you something in confidence. Only my confessor knows what I say to you now, so you must promise me that you will not tell anyone. Jesus and Our Lady manifest themselves and speak to me!

Do we want a definition of the mystical life? Here, this is the most beautiful definition: speaking heart-to-heart with God.

CHAPTER SEVEN

THE EVERYDAY MYSTIC

In everyday life, you adhere to God

WE HAVE SAID that Father Candido can, without a shadow of a doubt, be referred to with the title "mystic." The mystic is someone who is never far, never too far away, or unreachable. The mystic has the scent of the ordinary. In fact, he has the scent of the concrete life. And it is precisely in the concrete, everyday life that the continuous transformation of the lover into the Beloved takes place.[1]

Adherence to God takes place in everyday life; this very adherence represents the need to follow in the footsteps of Christ. Mysticism, as we said earlier, is part of being a Christian. Admiration is unanimous, in this regard, on the part of those who approached Father Candido.

His ability to listen was precious; his availability was affectionate and amiable. His extraordinariness lay in the singular ability to penetrate hearts and embrace the most varied experiences with selfless and total love. His striking humility and his consistent and wise teaching of love still captivate us today. All his actions were God-oriented; Father

---

[1] See, in this regard, the numerous references to what Karl Rahner calls "the mysticism of the everyday" and "the open-eyed mysticism."

Candido trusted only in the infinite merits of Jesus' Passion and in His mercy. Specifically, this is also why we can speak of a "mysticism of mercy." Father Candido lived this aspect to the full: he gave himself totally to his neighbor by giving himself totally to God. One could say that he understood what the philosopher Lévinas stated, namely, that the "voice of God is the face of one's neighbor." There is a δύναμις, a secret force, which gives depth and gusto to the little things of everyday life; and that is love. The Christian longs for Heaven; the Christian measures the value of things not on the immediate or on a common mentality, but on the perspective of eternity which is, then, the only valid one.

Away from fanaticism and empty devotionalism

Father Candido moves us to open the confines of our half-hearted faith and to explore the infinity of God! In the face of misleading proposals of life or spirituality; in the face of mystical exaggerations and fanaticism or empty *devotionalism*, this good priest is a sure guide for us who lived out his personal call to holiness in silence. He lived an intimacy and communion with the Trinity in striking simplicity, with that balance that we can call exactly "everyday mysticism."

The secret, as we have already said and will not tire of repeating, is contained in his having lived in full union with God, evident in every attitude, in his self-annihilation. Clearly, from here, we see his having been a transparent, devout, zealous, serene, balanced, trusting man of faith. Regarding charity, he never had enough. To the contemporary man and woman, Amantini restores and reminds us of the simple mysticism of the house of Nazareth: this is true Christian mysticism, to which we must all aspire; toward which we must all walk.

Father Candido was able to transform the dry bones of formulas into a living prayer that breathed and moved under the impulses of the Spirit. He silently injected hope into history and into the lives of men. His life was an effective witness to God's love among men.

Father Candido "lost" and offered time to God. He "lost" and offered his life to God for his brothers and sisters. He allowed himself to be contemplated by God, while he contemplated God. And this perfect union of his with Christ led him to *mystical* experiences, to infused contemplation. It is contemplation, moreover, that infuses the impetus toward all renunciations and all interests; it is contemplation that horrifies one's even slightest imperfections, and thus makes possible a fuller fusion of the soul with Christ.

CHAPTER EIGHT

THE LOVER OF MARY MOST HOLY

With the "Rosary" in hand

ALL BIOGRAPHERS, particularly those who study the lives of the saints, often highlight some particular aspect of the personage under consideration. I thought it necessary to dwell on our Servant of God's devotion to the Blessed Virgin.

Father Gabriele Amorth, Amantini's disciple, recalled several times that Father Candido was most devoted to Mary. Those who knew him recall that the Servant of God always had the rosary beads in his hand, even as he spoke. He often spoke about Our Lady and devotion to the Virgin of Lourdes was, above all, fervent in Amantini.

Mary Most Holy was *at* the center of his life, if not *the* center of his life. She was an ever-present figure who was able to show, gently, the way (*Odegitria*, to use the term given to her by our Eastern brothers and sisters in the Faith) to reach her Son Jesus.

Throughout the course of his life, several things emerge: his passionate love for God, for the Immaculate, and for the salvation of every man.

Imitating Mary, consecrating himself to her and her Immaculate Heart, day after day, was his personal path of sanctification. Our Lady was always in Father Amantini's heart, and he never tired of inculcating in his spiritual sons and daughters the love for the Mother of God and the need to "be all of Mary."

Total belonging to the Immaculate was, therefore, his "secret." It was a secret, however, that he did not wish to keep to himself and that would form the fulcrum of his entire ministry.

Amantini had profound and most singular expressions of devotion for the Blessed Virgin. In his book, *Il mistero di Maria* (*The Mystery of Mary*) there are remarkable ones. Here, I shall cite some of them:

> Mary by her perfection shortened the distance that separates the Creator from His creatures, and above all appeared to Heaven so filled with holiness and grace, as indeed the holy Ark and the living Temple of God must have been, that is, worthy indeed to house in herself Holiness by her essence.

> The sanctification of the Most Blessed Virgin, which flows from her divine Maternity, is far superior to any created capacity. It radically excludes all personal subjection to sin and even every abhorrent reflection of sin. It is because of this absolute singularity that She rises incomparably above us all.

> For this reason Mary is called by the Church the *Most Holy*. In her divine Maternity is the consummation of every grace and all essential glory, and we could not, without risking becoming sacrilegious, mark limitations on the Virgin's prestige.

Candido of the Immaculate

Father Candido, in his tormented sleepless nights, continually invoked the Immaculate whose name he bore: *Candido of the Immaculate*. This, in fact, was the name chosen for him back on October 23, 1929, when he received from his novice master, the Venerable Nazareno Santolini,[1] a new religious name and Passionist habit: Candido of the Immaculate, indeed. His love for the Virgin was well-rooted in a profound knowledge that became over time *acquaintance*, albeit spiritual. The only book he wrote, *Il mistero di Maria*

---

[1] I think it appropriate to say a word about Venerable Nazareno Santolini, whose memory is still alive in the Passionist Congregation. He was born in Caldarola (Macerata), to Domenico Santolini and Filomena Gualdi, on October 23, 1859 (according to his baptismal record). At the age of 12, on November 4, 1871, he was received into the Almo Collegio Capranica seminary in Rome (founded in 1450 by Cardinal Domenico Capranica). The foundation of his priestly formation was study and piety! He received his doctorate in Philosophy on July 16, 1878, and his licentiate in Theology on July 26, 1881. During a trip to Mount Cavo, south of Rome, with his fellow seminarians, he became inspired by the penitent and austere life of the small Passionist community founded there by St. Paul of the Cross on October 10, 1758. He suddenly interrupted his studies, and thus consequently also the brilliant ecclesiastical career that lay ahead, to follow God's call to religious life. He asked to be admitted to the Congregation as a brother *converso* [that is, a lay brother]. Blessed Silvestrelli, who welcomed him with paternal affection in the Retreat of the Holy Stairs, sensed that before him was a special and exceptional soul! Humble and detached. On Nov. 18, 1881, he donned the Passionist habit and took the name Confrere Nazareno of Mary Immaculate, because, as he would later write to his sister Silvia (Lett. XLVII p. 236), "To Our Lady, after God, we owe everything." On Nov. 18, 1882, he made his profession at the hand of Father Noberto, Consultor General, former director of St. Gabriel of Our Lady of Sorrows. On Dec. 23, 1882, he was ordained to the subdiaconate; the following Feb. 23, to the diaconate; and finally, the last stage, of a journey rich in graces, he was conferred priestly faculties on March 10. On June 6, 1893 before the close of the first session of the 40th chapter, he was appointed novice master. He would remain in that post until the end of his life. He died at the age of 70, rich in merit, on January 4, 1930. He was a humble man, already during his life he enjoyed saintly esteem: superiors, pupils, eminent figures such as Cardinal Laurenti and Pope Benedict XV had great affection and admiration for him. He remains in the history of the Congregation as "the Master" not only because of his 30-year tenure in that office as novice master, but because he was a model for many young people. St. John Paul II proclaimed him Venerable on September 7, 1989.

(*The Mystery of Mary*), bears witness to this. It is a dense and highly topical compendium of Mariology. In the 344-page text, the Servant of God illustrates the figure of Mary based on Sacred Scripture, Patristics, and ecclesiastical doctrine.

The sanctuaries of Lourdes and Loreto were beloved pilgrimage destinations for Amantini. Father Candido used to send the people he worked with there. Moreover, he often went, accompanying pilgrims and the sick. And so it was that in Lourdes and Loreto many of the sick under his care were delivered. Regarding these pilgrimages, we have a moving *Way of the Cross* meditated by him and recorded in his voice in 1987 (the fiftieth anniversary of his priestly ordination), the reflections of which were collected in 2012 in an easy-to-read booklet, edited by me, entitled *A piccoli passi, camminando verso il cuore trafitto del Crocefisso* (*In small steps, walking towards the pierced heart of the Crucifix*).

Regarding Lourdes, one cannot help but reference the Servant of God Maddalena Carini[2] and the deep friendship she had with the exorcist of the Holy Stairs.

Who was Maddalena Carini?

Maddalena Carini was born in Bereguardo (Pavia) on March 1, 1917, and she died in Sanremo (Imperia) on January 26, 1998. She was the first Italian woman miraculously cured at Lourdes and whose healing was officially recognized by the Church. She was afflicted with Pott's disease, tubercular peritonitis, angina pectoris, pernicious anemia, and trochanteritis in the right leg. This was the awful clinical situation of a girl in her early thirties, immobilized for fifteen years and miraculously cured by the "Beautiful Lady" on August 15, 1948. Maddalena herself recounted the miracle of her healing:

---

[2] On September 4, 2013, the Church of Sanremo officially opened her process of beatification.

On the afternoon of Saturday, August 14, as I prayed at the Grotto, I felt an unspeakable joy at the presence of the Blessed Virgin, next to Jesus and St. Joseph. The next day, Sunday, the 15th, I was taken from the Grotto to the square for the Eucharistic blessing. When the bishop imparted the blessing where I also was, I felt a tingling in my entire person. I felt entirely healed.

After being miraculously healed, she lived for another fifty long years in close union with God, dying, finally, in a reputation for holiness. The healing was certified by doctors and after a long process approved by the then-Archbishop of Milan, Cardinal Montini, who later became Pope Paul VI.

In 1957, she started the *Ave Maria Family* in Sanremo with the goal of formation and apostolate. Father Candido had a deep spiritual relationship with Maddalena Carini. Amantini went with her on pilgrimage to Lourdes several times. Father Candido also stayed in Sanremo on various occasions, in the company of Maddalena. It is said that the two spoke little, but prayed much together.

On various occasions, he confided to Father Amorth that

Maddalena never speaks out of turn. What she says is true, and what she foretells comes true.

The French philosopher and writer Simon Weil wrote:

In a perfect friendship, two friends have agreed to be two in one. Friendship is a miracle for which a person accepts to look from a distance without getting any closer to the person who is as necessary to him as bread.

Friendship, we know, is an affectionate and almost fraternal feeling that unites people into one and transforms the self into a *we*. Spiritual friendship, in this respect, is a path toward friendship with Christ because He is the true light and model summed up by the true words, "Love your neighbor as yourself."

Our Lady and Candido's work in exorcism

Most Holy Mary was with Father Candido during exorcisms. He felt her delicate maternal presence.

In his book *The Mystery of Mary*, Father Candido writes about the theme of exorcism and healings:

> Now, from our experiences we know properly this: that almost nothing else returns as much torment to Satan as the invocation of Mary's name. Ordinarily, the obsessed cannot even pronounce her name freely, despite how much effort they put into it. Then there are some Marian devotions that are evidently annoying to demons, since the obsessed can hardly ever practice them without a great deal of effort. These include the Hail Mary, the daily tribute of St. Bonaventure, and the rosary. The power of the Virgin in expelling demons from the bodies of the possessed is equally clearly demonstrated to us by the results obtained with constant Marian devotion. For by it, these come to change much for the better and even completely resolve the saddest conditions of this world. Those same particularly harsh and obstinate demons, who, as the Gospel tells us, do not yield except to extreme means, quickly languish in strength when they are faced with the special protection of the Virgin. Experience teaches that those who have had recourse to Her in similar situations with lively, filial devotion sooner or later emerge.

Sometimes, however, the evil one has been forced to confess, to his own shame, by the mouth of the obsessed, his complete impotence before the will of the Sovereign Lady of Heaven and Earth.

It is impossible to ignore, moreover, the large number of Miraculous Medals Father Candido gave to his faithful. Everyone who went to him came back with one hanging around his neck. His only ambition (I am not exaggerating) I think was always to work *for Mary* and *with Mary* for the Kingdom of God. He had, for this very reason, in the rosary, the suitable instrument to witness to his devotion and gratitude to the Mother of God. The rosary was the continuous nourishment of his contemplative life and his apostolic life. We can relate these words to the Servant of God:

> In the rosary, I am with You, I think with You, I look with You, I admire with You, I suffer with You, I weep with You, I hope with You, I love with You, O Mary, Teacher and Mother; You teach me to know Jesus closely and to love Him with simplicity, as in Nazareth. I need the simplicity of children to enter Heaven with You, O Mary. (Enrico Rossetti, *Pensieri Religiosi*) (*Religious Thoughts*)

Regarding the sorrows of the Blessed Mary, in the meditations for the *Way of the Cross* cited earlier, Father Candido said:

> St. John speaks to us of the Virgin at the foot of the Cross, and it was certainly a sad sight to think that a mother had stood beside her Son while he was being killed. And killed in such a way! On the Cross. And we should not think

that Our Lady was only at the foot of the Cross, appearing, then, almost suddenly. The Gospel recalls Her at that moment for a very great importance, because Jesus says to Her: "Woman, behold thy Son," and to John, "Son, behold thy Mother." Our Lady was associated with our Lord Jesus Christ [...] in the mystery of the Redemption. Not only Jesus, but also His Mother. We know that the Mother, Our Lady, is the highest expression, I would say, of the woman who came out of the hands of God; more than Eve, as we have said, but in the mystery of the Redemption she participated in it in an active way and she still participates in this mystery even from Heaven, like the Lord. She is always present, but she was also present there and had to be present with the martyrdom of her heart, that martyrdom that had already been revealed to her by the elderly Simeon when Our Lady presented Jesus in the Temple.

As many saints preferred to die with the rosary beads in their hands, requesting to continue to keep it wrapped around their hands even after death, Father Candido, on his deathbed, though unable to recite any long prayers, nevertheless held it tightly in his hand. It was consoling for him, I like to think, to die with the rosary in his hands, reciting it for the last time.

"If every day," said Blessed Columba Marmion, "we have often repeated to the Virgin, 'Mother of God, pray for us…now and at the hour of our death', when the instant comes when the 'now' and the 'hour of our death' will be one and the same moment, we will be sure that the Virgin will not abandon us."

How, then, can we summarize our Servant of God's devotion to the Blessed Virgin?

Father Candido's life was imbued with the tenderness of the heart of the Mother. Consecrating himself to this heart meant for him to return, every day, under the Cross which is, then, the fundamental core of the Gospel. Under the Cross, all evil that is both in the world and in man is annihilated. Marian devotion found a place in the priestly heart! It could not but be so!

His is a singular space that speaks of pain, patience, humility, offering, and sacrifice but nevertheless instills great hope.

CHAPTER NINE

THE HUMBLE AND PRUDENT MAN

The Saints, an open banquet for the small and the great

A TRUE EXPERIENCE of faith never asks the Gospel what it can keep of its own life and interests without renouncing them; a true experience of faith is capable of giving up everything to the point of considering everything that is not of Christ and His Gospel to be "rubbish" (see Philippians 3:8); a true experience of faith accepts "losing everything," it lives the grammar of love, not of calculation, of gratuitousness and total availability to the Gospel and Christ. This is what the saints have done.

A true experience of God is open to encountering: the saints are, in fact, figures in whom everyone can see himself, find consolation in his own sufferings, and receive ever new impulses to improve himself, so that all who wish may be drawn into God's orbit. The saints are a table open to little ones and adults alike, called to walk with rigor, but also with levity and gentleness, in the luminous and cruciform itinerary of faith. The saints are fountains from whom even those who are in the first steps of Christian sustenance can draw substantial nourishment. They are a sweet and not fully fermented *wine* intended, too, for those who *cannot yet become intoxicated.* The French writer Georges Bernanos notes that:

Holiness cannot be forced into one formula; rather, it can be summarized in all of them. It encompasses and exceeds all forces; it realizes the condensation, constricted into a single plane, of the highest human faculties.

Holiness touches everyone. The saints, radically-believing men and women, have passed through history dissatisfied with material things and with the world and have found their fulfillment in God. God, in fact, stirs and forms them. He has no patterns and, still today, His infinite imagination never ceases to amaze us. I believe then that it is necessary for Christians of today to become aware of the fact that encountering the saints can produce immeasurable inner enrichment.

In this society of *self-dissolution*, one which has lost its own reason for existing, returning to the saints also means awakening that unquenchable thirst for the infinite and for new holiness that dwells in the hearts of so many. Michael Baumgarten, wrote (prophetically) that

> there are times when discourses and writings are no longer enough to make the necessary truth generally understandable. In such times, the actions and sufferings of the saints must create a new alphabet to unveil anew the secret of truth.

Today,

> in a history of the Church that was truly a sacred history, that is, a history of what the Spirit is *working* in the Church and not simply a chronicle of events concerning people of the Church, hagiography should have a far more important place than it is currently accorded. We can rejoice that today there are

considerable historical, literary, and cinematic attempts, which tend toward having us relive the lives of the saints... (Adolfo Lippi, *San Paolo della Croce*[1])

This allows that holiness to help us enter into the rhythm of Divine Life, into the demands of faith, in order to be surprised by the workings of God!

I write about the saints because they are disliked by all those lobbies of theologians who debate the celibacy of priests, the virginity of Mary, and common-law and gay marriages. These so-called "progressive" theologians consider the saints ignorant and "passé" (that is, out of fashion). They are *too old* for the Church. The saints, on the contrary, are precisely those "simple people" who, by the Gospel, understand what is hidden from the learned and knowledgeable. For, as they teach us, returning to that genuine Tradition that formed them can be a remedy for this decaying world. In the "school of the saints," hence, we learn how to read our history as that of men and women who are not seduced by an overly disproportionate image of themselves. Parameters change, times change, and perhaps even modalities change, but holiness remains a possible and attainable experience!

Living by the Eucharist and "becoming" Eucharist

For Father Candido, to use an image, humility was the great insulator that allowed the divine current of grace to pass through his person without dissipating or provoking flare-ups of pride and rivalry. Father Candido was a religious and a priest who lived by the Eucharist and "became" Eucharist for his brothers and sisters. He lived his life with a heart spiritually turned to Heaven and the tabernacle! His spirituality and his entire ministry were centered in *Jesus-the-Host*: his prayers before the tabernacle were endless, his

---

[1] "St. Paul of the Cross"

Masses fervent, and his Communions devout. The Jesus he received in the sacramental sign of bread took him out among the holy people, whom he would have liked to have gathered devoutly before the tabernacle. At the foot of the tabernacle, he sincerely laid down not only all his own miseries, but also those of the people who asked him to be remembered in prayer, or the many stories, most often painful, of those he had met throughout the day.

We can say, without exaggeration, that Father Candido lived in a Eucharistic way; that is, he knew how to come out of himself, out of the narrowness of his own life, and he grew by drawing on the vitality of Christ. Some recount that, at times, he would open the tabernacle and, taking the pyx in his hands, he would broadly trace, in the silence of the night, the cross, thus blessing the entire world. At the feet of Jesus in the Sacrament, he placed all the sufferings of his brethren, whose sufferings he bore during the day. Before the Eucharist, he recharged his energies and filled up with God's Love and Mercy, of which he became a privileged channel for the Father's graces to descend like dew to his neediest children. The faithful flocked to his morning Masses, which he celebrated at the chapel of St. Sylvester — the "choir" of the Passionist friars.

Faith brings us into God's world and illuminates our lives. We are not "supermen," able to go through life without hardships. Life often spares no one its harshness. We learn to live by living; by living a life sometimes made up of failings, even serious ones; a life in which, despite everything, He continues to renew His trust and turn His encouraging gaze on us. He asks us, however, to turn our wounds into places and occasions for witness. He asks us to live that life capable of a "total surrender" — a definitive abandonment in Him, with all our wounded but redeemed humanity, as happens in the Eucharist, when He surrenders Himself entirely to us. This is knowing God, this is living eternal life from down here.

The centrality of the crucified Christ

We spoke earlier about the *knowledge of suffering*. Father Amantini's total acceptance of God's will, and his filial abandonment, led him to have the reference point of his life in the Cross. He lived united to Christ Crucified, always and forever Crucified. He understood that the knowledge of the saints is acquired on Calvary. This is why he always testified to the primacy of God, leaving a splendid example of charity and holiness that still resonates loudly in the Church today.

This was the experience of our Servant of God. His living heart-to-heart with God teaches us to be *little Eucharists* in the world.

Our existence is extroverted and very distracted. Amidst so much distraction and bewilderment, we hardly stop to reflect on issues of the spirit. We live in a world that increasingly resembles the one described by George Orwell; indeed, it is somewhere between the one described by Aldous Huxley in *Brave New World* and Big Brother, the fictional character created by Orwell, in his novel *1984*. We are surrounded by men, and perhaps a little like them ourselves, permanently devoted to consumerism, lost in the "obligation of *jouissance* (enjoyment)" — in the words of the French philosopher Jacques Lacan. They are men who have lost the moral compass of limitations and wander desperately in search of pleasure. Our society envisions *jouissance* as a duty, as an obligation, legislating that being a man simply means indulging in what one likes! Instead, at the heart of this humble Passionist friar's message is mercy, humility, and knowledge that one is loved and desired by Christ. It is a unique, great certainty!

The direction of souls and the art of prudence

Everyone agrees that Amantini was a great director of souls. He commendably practiced the cardinal virtue of prudence. He spoke only when questioned and when in need, always concisely, in a subdued and delicate tone of voice. He avoided following his natural instincts, but turned with filial confidence to God. He was a wise man, capable of judging with discernment and then acting faithfully and coherently. The Servant of God greatly valued rendering his entire life a meaning that corresponded to the divine desire.

One of the gifts we cannot deny Father Candido is that he consistently held to an objective view of the internal state of a soul on the spiritual journey. He demanded, however, that that trust he placed in the hearts of souls be supported by concrete acts and not pious wishful thinking. He was truly the man of formative suffering that affects and molds new men; the man of poverty that by singular privilege enriches the dignity of every man; he is the man of preaching who resounds the Truth that saves; he is the man who forms young people because he believes in the future; he is the man of prayer as the only means of responding to the Word of God; he is the man made solitude and silence to offer companionship and solidarity to every person.

CHAPTER TEN

THE REPUTATION OF HOLINESS!

Padre Pio, Father Candido, and holiness

THERE WAS a priest, who without ever having met Father Candido, already mysteriously knew everything about him: Saint Pio of Pietrelcina. Sometimes the faithful in Rome would go to him in San Giovanni Rotondo for confession or counsel and would receive an almost gruff reply, "But why don't you go to Father Candido?" St. Pio had such great esteem for him, so much so that he used to say, "You have a saint at the Holy Stairs!"

That common esteem is growing today, just as the number of pilgrims who come to visit his tomb housed at the Pontifical Sanctuary of the Holy Stairs is increasing.

There is nothing striking in Father Candido, as he did not accomplish great feats in the eyes of the world. He was a priest, only and always a priest, that is, an *alter Christus*. He was a man committed, day and night, to the salvation of souls. That is why, while he was still alive, he was surrounded by an extraordinary reputation of holiness.

I was able to personally attest to this, through so many sentiments of admiration on the part of those who knew him and beyond. The testimonies in this regard are numerous.

There are many, in fact, who affirm his sanctity. This reputation has never been tarnished; on the contrary, it has become more and more consolidated and extended not only among his confreres, who certainly had contact with him, even if not substantial, but more so in his many devout spiritual children. It is well known, then, that there are numerous people who not only have a holy and consoling memory of the Servant of God, but who resort to him in times of particular difficulty.

Antidote to despair

As is well known, his reputation of holiness "exploded" after his funeral, which was attended by multitudes of people. It then grew subsequently, extending well beyond Rome. Much is owed, in this regard, to Father Gabriele Amorth, who never ceased speaking about and always recalling his beloved teacher.

Many people, still today, visit Amantini's tomb and turn to him in intercession, seeking favor from God. He was and is an excellent "antidote to despair."

Father Candido celebrated the Holy Mass with ardor, heard confessions, administered the sacraments, preached, prayed, and *blessed.* Everything else was a waste of time for him and, above all, a waste of God. People, as well, looked to him for no other reason than the fact that he continued to point to God with his eyes imbued with tenderness and compassion, fatherly patience, and mercy. He did this to the very end; no one and nothing could turn him away from the altar and the confessional, from his life of union and intimacy with Jesus, of identification with Him — the high and eternal priest.

Chapter Eleven

Final Analysis

What do we need to be happy?

F R. CANDIDO reminded his spiritual children:

Jesus fulfilled everything through His death, because it was the Father's will that He atone through the immolation of Himself, until the end, atone for sin and bring salvation to us. Without the Lord's death, without Him offering Himself for humanity, no man could have had salvation, and even today no man can have salvation without living faith in Jesus Christ. Let us try to imitate the Lord, to thank Him for what He has done, but when we too must suffer our pains, our crosses, our obstacles, accept them and love them knowing that it is the Father's will that we also resemble Him. Let us remember one thing, that we must always meditate on what the Lord said to His Apostles, "It is not you who have sought Me, but it is I who have sought you," and at another point, "No one comes to Me unless the Father draws him to Me," and to His Apostles, in His prayer to the Father after the institution of the Eucharist, after predicting to His Apostles that His Passion would begin that night, He prayed to the Father in this way: "Father, those whom You gave Me I have kept; I pray to You for them and not only for them, but also for those who hereafter, throughout the ages, will believe their words and believe in Me." And the Lord, "It is not we who have gone to seek Him, it is He who has called us. 'No one comes to Me unless the Father draws him to Me'." It is the Father who brought us to the Lord, it is the Father who gave us faith, and we have to live this faith, keep faithful to this vocation that is the greatest gift the Lord could give us. When the Apostle Paul, the Apostle Peter, and all the other Apostles went throughout the world to preach, St. Paul said, "Those were converted to whom the Spirit opened their hearts to hear what Peter said and what all the other Apostles said." We have believed Christ; to this day we have been chosen. In ancient times, there was the Chosen People; that people prevailed, we heard what the high priests say, the leaders of the people of Israel, under the Cross; they scorn Christ, they mock Christ, they turn away from Him. And God, in His mercy, chooses among all the nations, all the other peoples without distinction. Before, they were the chosen people, and there was not — Scripture says — a people who had God as close as Israel, as the Jews. Now [...] in their place, the Lord has placed us. We are the chosen people. We are the Church and this Church has been chosen by the Heavenly Father, and we have received the fruit of the

Blood of Christ. (Meditations from the *Way of the Cross*).

These moving words of his remind us that the Gospel is something (or rather Someone) to be believed in, not so much because of fear of a terrible outcome, but rather because it has gathered and is gathering, every day, that deepest longing proper to the heart of every man — a longing for fulfilled humanity, communion, and sharing!

Otherwise, one would wonder why the Gospel still exerts so much attraction.

We are not happy except when we open our hearts and let God, His Word, breach our lives. Today we have and possess everything!

Yet, in spite of this, there is always a shadowy area in our hearts, where we feel that although we have everything, we always need that extra something to be happy.

Eternal life remains "lurking"

Father Candido allowed himself to be shaken and captivated by Him, allowing himself to be shared, in solidarity, and in communion; he was, day after day, moment after moment, rooted in Him, by preparing a space in his heart, a space that would become prayer and longing! He made his life a ceaseless preaching of the beauty of his own consecration to the Lord, a preaching to which was added the proposal, or rather the invitation, to listen to the Lord's voice and follow it.

He taught us that eternal Life (perennially) remains "lurking" behind the miserable affairs of humanity, also wounded — like Jesus.

His eyes, sky-colored and Heaven-impregnated, reminded us that Heaven is not just the dream of children who make their First Communion, but the absolutely real happiness for which we were all created and redeemed.

And now that he is there, beside Him, may he continue to pray for this world of ours plagued by an efficiency-based progressivism, where a democracy without truth dominates, making the concept of charity increasingly incomprehensible; in this world where the idea that "either you dominate or you are dominated" reigns undisturbed, may he remind us that the essential is God and that everything, even the most necessary, collapses before His boundless love.

Confronting the mystery of the crucified God

In summarizing his message, one would say that this very humble priest taught us that if a Christian desires to learn how to pray, he must necessarily confront the mystery of Christ Crucified — after all, therein lies the newness of the Gospel; a newness that fertilizes faith and transforms it into Trinitarian faith, which introduces us into the mystery of the heart of the Father.

Prayer, he reminded us, is that "hook" thrown to Heaven; it guides us by unknown paths, by roads that suddenly open in the midst of the deserts of our lives. Through prayer, God, in fact, teaches us the right path by taking us by the hand, and is moved as a father is at every tiny step toward holiness!

Thank you, beloved Father, because the only thing that counts, in the confusion of the world, is the Word of the Gospel. A Word that shows a path, a road to travel; a life to live.

It forces us, each day, to review our lives and our patterns, our mental settings. We spend time, at times, flipping through the Gospel, perpetually seeking new "excitement" and end up, as always, no longer recognizing it as the *Word* that saves. Patience and waiting: these should be, as they were for him, the tracks on which to walk: patience in seeking and waiting for an answer! For only if we begin to patiently search in every line of the Gospel will we find what we are looking for!

The Christ announced by our Servant of God is the totally open *New Man* in whom the walls of His life are broken down, so that He is integrally a "passageway"; He is the New Man made "passageway." The future of man, of every man, of total man, depends on the Cross; but more still: *the redemption of man is the Cross.*

And no man will truly become himself in any other way, except by allowing the breaking down of the walls of one's life: the walls of pride, presumption, and sin, thus being able to turn one's gaze to the *Pierced One*, called by a new name; to follow the One who opened the way to the future.

This was the life of the man Eraldo Ulisse Mauro Amantini.

This was the ministry of the exorcist-priest, Candido of the Immaculate.

This was the prophecy of the "saint."

APPENDIX

WORDS OF FATHER GABRIELE AMORTH REGARDING FATHER CANDIDO AMANTINI[1]

I N 1986, my life changed. I had had a very lighthearted rapport with Cardinal Poletti, because by nature I am a joker.

One afternoon in June of that year, I decided to pay him a visit, so I called on him at his home, intending to offer him some cheerful company. He came to the door himself, and during our conversation he mentioned Father Candido Amantini, the exorcist at the Scala Santa at the Basilica of Saint John Lateran. "You know Father Candido?" he asked me. "Yes," I responded. And he said to me: "Since he is ill, he has much need of an assistant." And I said: "But, you know me, I am a joker, a good-for-nothing, good only for telling jokes and playing pranks....No way!"

---

[1] Collected by Elisabetta Fezzi and published in *Padre Amorth. La mia lotta con Dio contro Satana*, San Paolo, 2017. We believe we are doing an important service to the reader by including these texts that bear witness to the relationship between two of the most significant figures in the exorcism ministry in Italy (the third is certainly Father La Grua, whose work, published by Edizioni San Paolo, in Italian, in what is a true "spiritual testament": *La mia lotta contro il maligno. Vita di padre Matteo La Grua (My Struggle with God against the Evil One, The Life of Father Matteo La Grua)*, Roberta Ruscica, 2017). (Ed: This Appendix is translated by Bret Thoman for the English edition.)

I was aware, however, that there was nothing I could do! So I commended myself to Our Lady, asking in prayer, "Protect me under your mantle, and I shall be secure!" Many times after, the Devil said to me: "We can do nothing to you; you are too protected!" And so I am; I am protected under the mantle of Our Lady! And thus, in 1986, I became an exorcist.

My great grace was that I was appointed as an exorcist by Cardinal Poletti to assist Father Candido Amantini, a saintly and famous exorcist whom I had as a teacher for six years. My great good fortune was that, because I also started from scratch, I knew absolutely nothing.

With Father Pio and Father Candido against the devil

Padre Pio died in 1968 and I was appointed in 1986. Yet, he was close to me when I needed him! During exorcisms several times the devil, through the person exorcised, said, "Away with that friar, I don't want that friar!" "Who is he? Padre Pio?" "Yes, it's him, I don't want him!" He was present! Just as many other times Father Candido was present. "Away with that priest! Away with that priest!" he shouted. "Who is he? Father Candido?" "Yes, yes it's him!" Well, if the two of them are with me when I do exorcisms, I'm in pretty good shape! [...]

I had gone to the Holy Stairs a few times, and I had met Father Candido there and talked to him. I knew him, but not that much, I hardly knew him. Then instead for six years we were together, inseparable.

Well, Cardinal Poletti gave me a great gift because he immediately appointed me as an exorcist with full powers even though I was under Father Candido's service, so I had to obey him without question. The first thing Father Candido said to me was, "Start [learning the ritual] right away in your house!" Then I would go to him, we would do some together, chat, discuss the various cases...

Father Candido used to say, "It is useless to perform long exorcisms, at any rate, if it is not the time set by the Lord..." And in fact, several times the devil, when questioned under exorcism, foretells the date he will go away. The problem is that he is a liar. Once, he mocked me; he really mocked me because, in the case just mentioned, he foretold that he would leave a person's body precisely on the Feast of the Immaculate Conception, which did not happen. So later I asked him, "Why did you not leave [the person]?" He replied, "Didn't they teach you that I am a liar, didn't they ever tell you that I don't tell the truth?"

He really cheated me, I felt I was fooled by the devil! True, he is a liar, however, sometimes he is forced by God to tell the truth, and then on that day and at that time he really comes out. I had an episode with a farmer who was about twenty-six or twenty-seven years old. It was a terrible case. I had a Franciscan friar minor named Brother Sebastian to assist me, plus three or four other very strong people to hold him down. He even levitated during the exorcism. He always spoke in English, I didn't understand, but I had those who translated for me, and he immediately said, "I am Lucifer." You have to know that saying the name, for the devil, is a serious defeat. In this case, he immediately revealed his name. And he said, "I will leave on June 21 at 11:00." We started exorcisms in February, had several meetings and then I gave him an appointment after June 21. At that time, I found the farmer perfectly free. I asked him, "What time were you set free?" He replied, "At exactly 11:00." I asked him again, "How did you realize this?" He replied, "I was in the countryside alone, I think I let out a big scream, but I'm not sure." To be on the safe side, I exorcised him a few more times, because sometimes there are temporary deliverances: the demon goes away temporarily, hoping that the person, a little at a time, will leave the Church and maybe return to a life of sin, and then he will get him back. And in this case, it is worse than before!

I am afraid of temporary deliverances; I am also afraid of fake or false deliverances. Sometimes the demon pretends to go away, but I still continue to exorcise for a while. I don't usually do a prayer of thanksgiving for the deliverance that has taken place unless at least one year has passed. Father Candido always told me, "Do not expect to see the demon leave at the end of the exorcism and everyone goes away happy: do not expect this! He only goes away when the Lord has determined! It is He who has His plans; it is He who works!" In this case, the demon communicated the date and kept it even though the person was not under exorcism.

Some evidence of Father Candido

I have never been afraid, not even at the beginning! Never! I always say that it is the Devil who is afraid of me. I have said several times on television: "When the Devil sees me, he poops his pants!" In the beginning, I was with Fr. Candido who had my back. Then I made an iron pact with Our Lady! The Devil told me many times: "We cannot do anything to you, because you are too protected." I have my guardian angel, I have St. Gabriel, my namesake, and I have the mantle of the Madonna! I feel like a nobleman, always safe! I have a lot of help from up there, but the ones just mentioned are the foundation. Wrapped in Mary's mantle, I have no fear. I never even had troubles, while Fr. Candido did. Fr. Candido was a Passionist and worked at the Holy Stairs. Once, he was away from Rome and one of his confreres arrived unannounced. So they put him up in his room. The next day, Fr. Candido returned and his brother priest asked him: "How can you sleep in this room? There are constant noises, constant noises..." He replied: "I don't mind!" He would arise every night and go to the chapel for an hour of Adoration. Fr. Candido was a man of great prayer! I found out from someone who was aiding him that he was attacked by the Devil in his final moments: he stiffened and became serious and severe.

Well, we don't know how we are going to die! We pray over and over for a reason, "Pray for us sinners now and at the hour of our death." These are the two important moments of life, the present moment and the moment of death. We really need Our Lady's help!

An Unexpected Lesson in Theology

I remember a lesson the devil once gave Father Candido. While he was liberating a person, he said to the demon, "Go on, the Lord has prepared for you a nice little house that is well-heated, in which you will never suffer from cold, in which you will always be very warm..." And the devil said imperiously, "You do not know anything!" When he interrupts by saying, "You don't know anything, you don't understand anything," it means that the Lord has commanded him to teach the exorcist a lesson, which is, "He is not the one who created Hell!" It means that God created only good things. "It was us [who created Hell], He had not even thought about it," the devil continued, "It was not in God's plans that Hell existed!"

That Hell was created by demons is not found in any Theology book, but neither is it said in any book that God created it. This is never found.

What an incredible lesson for someone like Father Candido who taught Theology, Sacred Scripture, and more!

On those who rely too much on charisms

I fight against these things; Father La Grua also fought against them. It's maniacal! Yes, it's maniacal! It happens because people believe that they have, more or less consciously, powers. We have only the power to pray! Father Candido used to say, "I'm not against [charismatic] prayer groups, but then in the end everyone has powers, everyone has charisms... they are all charismatic!"

That is, there is a risk that, perhaps after witnessing some prayers of deliverance in a prayer group that are done well and yield results, everyone feels that they can do it their way, *"alla carlona"* [that is, carelessly].

Even prayers of deliverance have to be done well: and one of the ways to do them well is to keep your hands still. At most I say, raise your hand toward the person you are praying for, but nothing more. I have preached to many charismatic renewal groups and I have always spoken clearly about this; but then some do what they want, because they get exalted up there, too. The risk there is that one exalts himself, that he believes he has powers he does not have.

A blessing

This is [...] the blessing that I call Father Candido's, because he and I always exchanged it:

> May the Lord Jesus be with you always.
> May He walk before you to guide you,
> May He be behind you to protect you,
> May He dwell within you to guard you,
> May He be above you to enlighten you.
> Amen.

However, I offer it in Latin because, who knows why, demons fear Latin more than Italian: it must be because it is the official language of the Church!

> *Dominus noster Jesus Christus, apud nos sit ut nos defendat,*
> *intra nos sit ut nos conservet, ante nos sit ut nos ducat,*
> *post nos sit ut nos custodiat,*
> *super nos sit ut nos benedicat, liberet et sanctificet:*

Qui cum Patre et Spiritu Sancto vivit et regnat in saecula saeculorum. Amen."

ABOUT THE AUTHOR

Andrea Maniglia (Monteroni di Lecce, 1988) obtained a Bachelor's degree in Theology from the Pontifical University of St. Thomas Aquinas (Angelicum) in Rome, as well as a Licentiate in Theology with a specialization in Theological Anthropology and a Doctorate in Theological Anthropology (conducting research on the Mariology of the Calabrian theologian Stefano De Fiores, 1933–2012) from the Pontifical Theological Faculty Teresianum in Rome. He is a Religion teacher for the Archdiocese of Milan and collaborates with various Catholic journals. He has authored several publications of a hagiographic nature.

Slaying Dragons Press

Slaying Dragons Press, founded in 2021, is the fruit of a spiritual work begun in 2016 which sought to find new ways to bring people the joy and beauty of the Catholic Faith. By God's Providence, what began under the name *The Retreat Box* has grown into *The Slaying Dragons Apostolate* and *Slaying Dragons Press*.

This work is a grassroots apostolate which thrives on support and endorsements from those who enjoy these books. As a result, fans of the books and supporters of the mission help increase the reach of *Slaying Dragons Press* by telling friends, family, priests, religious, and Bishops about these books.

Please consider supporting this work in any way that you can. While *Slaying Dragons Press* is *not* a non-profit, financial support is always welcome. Please visit SlayingDragonsPress.com for ways to support this apostolate. If you do not have a copy of the other celebrated books we have published, get one today!

Support this work on **Patreon**
~patreon.com/**theslayingdragonsapostolate**

Subscribe to our website for discounts and news
~SlayingDragonsPress.com/pages/**Subscribe**

Other Titles
from
Slaying Dragons Press

Slaying Dragons: *What Exorcists See & What We Should Know*, by Charles D. Fraune [1]

The Rise of the Occult: *What Exorcists & Former Occultists Want You to Know*, by Charles D. Fraune

The Occult Among Us: *Exorcists and Former Occultists Expose the Nature of This Modern Evil*, by Charles D. Fraune

Slaying Dragons - Prepare for Battle: *Applying the Wisdom of Exorcists to Your Spiritual Warfare*, by Charles D. Fraune
- (a study guide, manual, and companion book to Slaying Dragons)

Swords and Shadows: *Navigating Youth Amidst the Wiles of Satan*, by Charles D. Fraune [2]

Come Away By Yourselves: *A Guide to Prayer for Busy Catholics*, by Charles D. Fraune

The Life of St. Alphonsus Liguori, by a Member of the Order of Mercy (1886)

---

[1] Also available in Spanish and Portuguese.
[2] Also available in Spanish.

A Christian's Rule of Life *(with Darts of Fire),* by St. Alphonsus Liguori

Novena to the Holy Spirit: *Prayers and Meditations in Preparation for Pentecost,* by St. Alphonsus Liguori

Sanctifying Pregnancy: *In the Light of the Joyful Mysteries of the Rosary,* by Margaret Place (1954)

The Scourge of Demons: *A Classic Manual (1576) on Exorcism and Spiritual Warfare,* by Fr. Girolamo Menghi, OFM

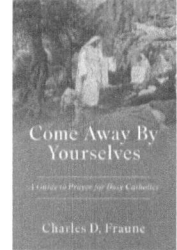

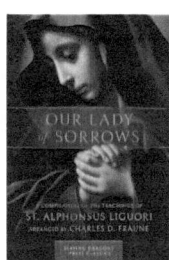

Slaying Dragons Press